Braving the Fire

ALSO BY JESSICA HANDLER

Invisible Sisters: A Memoir

Braving the Fire

A Guide to Writing About Grief and Loss

JESSICA HANDLER

St. Martin's Griffin ☙ New York

www.stmartins.com

Design by Patrice Sheridan

LIBRARY OF CONGRESS CATALOGING-IN-PUBLICATION DATA
AVAILABLE UPON REQUEST.

ISBN 978-1-250-01463-4 (trade paperback)
ISBN 978-1-250-01455-9 (e-book)

St. Martin's Griffin books may be purchased for educational, business, or promotional use. For information on bulk purchases, please contact Macmillan Corporate and Premium Sales Department at 1-800-221-7945, extension 5442, or write specialmarkets@macmillan.com.

First Edition: December 2013

10 9 8 7 6 5 4 3 2 1

Copyright Acknowledgments

To my family

Contents

Acknowledgments

Thanks to my steadfast writing group: Beth Gylys, Sheri Joseph, Peter McDade, and Susan Rebecca White, to The Josef and Anni Albers Foundation, and the Georgia State University Library. Thanks to Gabriella Burman and Adam Kaplan, Candler Park Yoga, Tracy Crow, Jay Edwards, Beth Lilly, Brian Mahoney, Claudya Muller, Amy Rogers Nazarov, Paige Oliver, Ginger Pinholster. Thanks to Kathryn Rhett for naming the whispering tribe. Boundless thanks to my agent, Sorche Fairbank, and her marathon listening skills, and to my editor, Daniela Rapp, ever calm. As always, thank you to my mother, Miriam Handler, who proved to me every day how much life there is beyond that not-so-secret club, and to my husband, Mickey Dubrow, without whom I can make no journey, large or small.

Introduction

TRANSFORMED BY LOSS

You may be holding this book because you have been changed by experiencing a great loss. Perhaps you're browsing these pages because you've been thinking that you want to write about what's happened to you, and you're wondering how to start. Perhaps you want to write about the ways that grief came into your life and what has happened in its aftermath, or you want to commemorate a loved one or way of life that's gone. After you've survived the death of a loved one, an illness, a broken romance, the loss of a home, country, or even a social structure, the story of who you are changes. In writing about what's changed, you want to make sense of the impact of your loss, or record life-altering events for yourself and for family and friends, including those not yet born. You already know that you're not alone in experiencing loss. You're also not alone in wanting to write about it. You may not know this yet, but you're also searching for a way to write about yourself as the memory keeper: the survivor of loss.

Like you, I'm someone with a personal story of loss and of

struggling to understand who I became after grief changed me. Years before I knew I would write my memoir *Invisible Sisters*, I searched for books that would help me find a way to write about my experience of loss. As far as I knew, "how-to" books about grief writing didn't exist: I would have to teach myself by following others' examples. I wanted honest, interesting memoirs about grieving, and approachable, welcoming books written from the perspective of the seriously ill person and her family, expressing the intimacies, paradoxes, and anger that come with living in a changed body and in a changed life. I was desperate for good books that proved that I wasn't alone in the journey my family and I had made: a journey that left me as the surviving sister of three.

How did other writers construct their stories, I wondered. What did they deem too personal, too technical, too distracting? What were the stellar details that made their writing exceptional? I was searching for a roadmap to understanding my grief, and eventually, how to write well about it.

My mother wanted books like these, too. She found inadequate reflection of her experience parenting two terminally ill children—my younger sisters—in medical narratives accessible to the layperson. She read *Eleven Blue Men* by Berton Roueché, and *The Lives of a Cell* by Lewis Thomas. I dipped into those books, but as a preteen, the writing style and word choices sometimes wavered in front of me, fascinating, terrifying, true—and intellectually and emotionally out of my reach. I read *The Diary of a Young Girl*, by Anne Frank, and was haunted by Anne's authentic teenage life, with its romantic crushes and keen self-inquiry even in the closest of quarters. My trials were not like hers, but I read that famous diary searching for clues to how to make a record of life lived in shadow.

I was an adult before I felt ready to write my family's story in earnest, and by then there were bright signposts for my journey: Lucy Grealy's memoir of growing up disfigured as a result of a facial tumor, *Autobiography of a Face*, and Joan Didion's memoir of her first year after the sudden death of her husband,

The Year of Magical Thinking. I read Virginia Woolf's *On Being Ill* and C. S. Lewis's *A Grief Observed.* Each of these books told a compelling story, welcomed me into a portion of the author's life, and showed me the strength and clarity I would need in order to write well about my love for and loss of my two sisters, and about the life I learned to live after their deaths.

At first I didn't recognize the amount of writing I had already done. I'd begun writing my way into my story years earlier, in the journals I began in elementary school and continue to this day. On those pages I recorded the quotidian moments of my life and my sisters' lives, small details that kept them forever as people: flawed, funny, and beloved. Other parts of our family's chronicle existed in the photographs, report cards, and letters that my mother kept. But the crux of the story was almost too painful to write. I had survived, but my sisters and our family as a unit had not.

Searching for guidance in others' stories of loss, I looked for writing lessons and I sought encouragement. Telling my story was the right thing to do for me and for my family, but before I could do that, I wanted proof that others had accomplished the daunting task of writing through their grief. Writing about truly painful subjects, like death, illness, divorce, war—anything that deeply changes your life—is as brave as holding a hand over a flame that's already burned you once. I knew it would hurt, but in order to write clearly about what happened and understand what my losses meant to me, I had to examine my story closely. If I could feel the good and bad moments again, maybe I could find an unforgettable way to describe that fire and how I came away from it.

I often speak to survivors' groups and writing clubs about my own experience of writing through grief. The attendees are eager to know how to capture on paper the stories that their loved ones can no longer tell, or to understand how to shape their own stories. They know that they possess that important reason to write, but they don't yet know if they have the courage.

Once, when I spoke to a bereavement group about my family's story, a man from the audience stayed close by me during the reception. He was elegantly dressed, and I could see by how he hung his head and the tentative way he approached me that he was haunted by his grief. His shoulders were bent as if he carried a tangible burden, and he seemed to have a well of questions he couldn't begin to ask. He told me his teenaged son had recently been killed in an accident. His wife, he said, was getting along better than he was—he gestured toward a vivacious woman talking with friends across the room—but he wasn't sure where to begin.

I knew what he wanted to ask me. How do I get past this, he would have asked. How can I be who I am now: a father who has buried his son?

You start by writing it down, is my answer to him here. Don't expect beautiful prose yet, to undo the terrible thing that has happened to bring you here, or even a million-dollar book deal. Simply tell your story and your son's story, and you will begin to build a bridge that connects who you were then with who you have become.

No story of loss is a simple one. The feelings that come with grief can be hard to pin down with a pen or put in order with a keyboard. As you write, you encounter strong emotions, memories, often a wealth of family stories, differing opinions, and facts. This is why writing about grief in steps helps you build that bridge.

Many people are aware that grieving can be seen as a series of stages, which is why I've drawn a parallel between writing about grief and one of the most well-recognized studies of grieving, the "Five Stages of Grief" by Dr. Elisabeth Kübler-Ross.

The Five Stages of Grief were introduced to the American public in 1969 with the publication of *On Death and Dying*. This short book by Dr. Kübler-Ross surveyed the results of her experiences discussing the end of life with terminally ill patients. From her study, she developed a five-stage model that she believed described the ways that the dying face their own grief and loss. She named the stages "Denial," "Anger," "Bargaining," "Depression," and "Acceptance." Over time, her model was adapted to address the ways that survivors cope, recognizing that the order of the stages may differ for each person, and that some people may not experience every stage. I'm one of many who don't believe that these stages always occur in a linear, rigid order, but I do believe that as a survivor of loss, I moved naturally through phases in an order that made sense for me. As a writer and as a person affected by grief, I haven't spent a lot of time in "Denial," but I've repeated "Depression" more than once.

Kübler-Ross wasn't the only person to study how we grieve. Some say that we experience grief in waves. Another theory proposes that living with grief requires of the survivor a series of tasks acknowledging their pain, and helping to form a new way of living without the loved one's presence. Religious practices also provide guidance in how to grieve: Roman Catholics anoint the sick toward the end of their lives, Jews sit shiva, Muslims place the deceased in their graves facing Mecca. Each of these are in their own way part of the story of surviving a loss.

But grief is never over. No matter how we grieve, we don't arrive at a neatly categorized, comfortably furnished place that some people like to call "closure." There isn't closure, really. We don't want to forget or be forgotten. We want to develop the ability to celebrate what we love as we move forward, even if that dear person, place, or thing is no longer actively in our lives. This is why I've added a sixth stage of my own to the five stages of grief. In that sixth stage, "Renewal," you have written that essential story that led you to pick up this book. You've built the bridge between who you were and who you have become.

Many writers have gone across that bridge before you. Their experiences and the ways in which they chose to write about their loss shine a light on your path. In this book, we'll examine techniques from well-regarded memoirs, and read insights from critically acclaimed authors who have written honestly and memorably about their own losses. At the end of each chapter, you'll find a section called "The Next Step," with craft exercises designed specifically for the writer of a memoir about grief or loss.

Moving through the stages in this book, we will examine the style and feeling with which Nick Flynn writes of his father's alcoholism and homelessness in *Another Bullshit Night in Suck City*. We'll look at the techniques Robin Hemley uses to write about immersing himself in second chances in *Do-Over!* We will consider how Janisse Ray expresses the importance of the natural world in two of her memoirs, *Drifting into Darien: A Personal and Natural History of the Altamaha River* and *Ecology of a Cracker Childhood*. How does a writer examine the way that their own or someone else's behavior creates grief? A look at Neil White's memoir of his time in prison, *In the Sanctuary of Outcasts*, and Sue William Silverman's exploration of childhood sexual abuse in *Because I Remember Terror, Father, I Remember You* will help illuminate the answers to that question. We'll discuss the ways that a journalistic approach helped Ethan Gilsdorf shape his memoir *Fantasy Freaks and Gaming Geeks*, and how United States poet laureate Natasha Trethewey found a place for facts and speculation in her memoir, *Beyond Katrina: A Meditation on the Mississippi Gulf Coast*. I've interviewed many of these authors about how and why they wrote their books. Their insights are shared in these pages.

These are just a few of the authors we'll examine who write nonfiction about loss, a subject addressed throughout history by greats like Michel de Montaigne, Virginia Woolf, Primo Levi, and Elie Wiesel. You are already part of a community of writers who have navigated their paths through loss, going back through the ages. Not all of the memoirs we'll examine on these pages are purely about grief or loss, although loss plays a part in almost everyone's story. I include some works here purely out of admiration for the author's beautiful language, captivating writing, or bracing approach to difficulty.

You are invited to use this book in any way that's helpful to you. You're welcome to see this as a guide to recognizing your feelings of grief and the ways they may have changed over time. Acknowledging a loss and its effect is often what inspires a writer to begin a memoir of grief. Your memoir may be done or nearly done, and you're simply interested in how to craft the best ending you can, or how to present a character at their idiosyncratic best. On the other hand, perhaps you're in the pre-writing stage and are just now examining how and why you want to write your story. No matter where you are in your writing journey, these chapters can be read as a linear, step-by-step guide to writing through grief, or as pages that you can dip in and out of to learn about other writers' experiences and examine some of their work. The tips and exercises are here for you to use as you like.

This book won't tell you how to get an agent, how to plan your book tour, or what kind of pencil to use when you scribble your ideas for your next book. What I hope is that this book will help you write your way through your grief and into renewal. Consider this book a guide to finding your way through the very personal journey of writing a true story that's hard to tell and impossible to forget.

MY STORY:

By the time I was thirty-two years old, I was the only one of three sisters still alive. This is the simplest way to explain my own story of grief. But there's so much more to say: that my sister Susie, eight years old when I was ten, died of leukemia and that my sister Sarah, four at the time, lived another twenty-three years with a rare and fatal blood disorder, knowing that she would die young, too. Our lives were normal, middle-class American kids' lives, except for those times when they weren't. At nine, I identified myself to doctors as "the well sibling." I had already formed an identity shaped by impending loss.

When Sarah was a young adult, she spoke casually for the first time about something we had never said aloud: that after her death, I would be the only one left. It would be up to me to remember my sisters and our lives together.

Of course I would not forget her; she was my little sister. But telling her story after she was gone seemed too daunting a task. And telling my own story as the survivor? I didn't yet understand how I would approach that. First, I would have to understand who I became when I was, in her words, "the only one left" of three sisters. Time would wear away our connections to friends and extended family, and some day, no one would know who my sisters had been. The responsibility was clear. Capturing our lives and holding them for myself, our friends, family, and perhaps people who never knew us would fall to me.

Sarah wanted to be remembered. I know this because she told me. Susie would have said the same thing. But when I wrote my memoir, *Invisible Sisters*, it was more than a *memento mori*, a reminder of mortality. I wrote it to tell my family's story, the good parts and the bad: to capture my youthful terror in waking late at night and hearing my father bundle Susie out of bed and rush her to the hospital for what would be the last time, or my joy in giggling with Sarah over our teenaged secrets. I also wrote *Invisible Sisters* to help myself understand the girl I had been and the woman I became. Writing was my search to remember myself as much as it was to remember my sisters.

My grief is bigger than a single event. Yours may be, too. It wasn't until after Sarah died that I decided I was ready to visit Susie's grave. I hadn't seen it in more than two decades, and this second death had to come before I felt ready to confront the first. Grief had spread across our family like ripples on a pond: our father had never fully recovered from Susie's death, our parents' marriage broke apart, and before I was out of my teens, I left home. I fought my jagged memories of the day Susie was buried, but I knew that if I was going to move forward, I would have to confront what I'd left behind.

Time had surrounded the cemetery with strip malls and a freeway. I walked the still-beautiful, green, manicured grounds, heading to the gentle slope where long ago I had sat in a folding chair at Susie's funeral. But when I got to the spot, there was no marker at all, just a mossy patch in the grass: one more heartbreak. The cemetery director told me that no marker had ever been purchased. Because I was by then older than my father had been the day he bought this grave, I understood that he had been too stunned to buy a marker that day or on the one-year anniversary of her death, traditionally the date in Judaism for placing a gravestone. My mother, too, had been consumed by the loss, and poured her energy into keeping the remaining family's lives moving forward.

So I did what they were unable to do. I bought a gravestone. Susie's grave now has a bronze plate with her name, her birth and death dates, and a Jewish blessing. With time, I had come to see that while my sister's unmarked grave was tragic in its own way, it was the *story* of this neglected grave that fascinated me. I wanted to know more about this family—*my* family—who had lost one child and knew they would lose another, and couldn't permit themselves to look backward for fear of never going forward again.

Looking back, I began to see that my parents' inability to face their grief and complete their middle daughter's memorial was similar to the first stage in Dr. Elisabeth Kübler-Ross's famous "Five Stages of Grief," "Denial."

Loss transforms the stories that we expected of our lives. We are no longer who we used to be, and our lives no longer work entirely as planned. Two weeks after my friends Genevieve and Ari's third child was born, their oldest child, Michaela, five years old and disabled since birth, died unexpectedly in her sleep. They were bereft, and one of the many challenges they faced after Michaela's death was learning to see themselves as the parents of two beloved typical children. Their lives were suddenly absent the requirements of their special-needs daughter, who first shaped their identities as parents. Genevieve, a journalist, changed her computer password to reflect her dead daughter's name. "Writing her name and seeing it in print is proof of her existence," she told me.

Almost all memoirs are ultimately about identity: who we once were, and who we have become. For author and editor Dinty W. Moore, a key question for a memoir writer to ask herself is who is she now after her identity changed as a result of the fire ignited by her grief? His use of "fire" as an image surprised me when we talked, because it's exactly how I think of change, too. Grief is a fire that's burned you once, maybe even more than once. In order to write about it, though, you have to hold your hand over that fire again. Our characters— and in memoir, they are us—are looking for a way to become who they must be now.

"What surprised me," Genevieve remembers about her daughter's death, "was how quickly the world went from real to unreal. Everything seemed like I was looking through fractured glass."

What strikes me most about Genevieve's metaphor of fractured glass is the idea that what we can see through those shards are the small moments, the details that don't at first seem to fit together to form a whole. But it's those details, even as broken pieces, that you put together to create a story that's about your unique experience of loss. Anyone can tell you that they're heartbroken or sad, and they would be telling the truth. But what if that "fractured glass" meant writing about getting the leash down from the hook by the back door and walking your dog for the last time, or the way your mother's car keys feel in your pocket the day you told her she could no longer drive? These are the small details that demonstrate great emotions. A remarkable example is the way in which Jean-Dominique Bauby wrote *The Diving Bell and The Butterfly,* his extraordinary memoir of almost total paralysis after a stroke that resulted in "locked-in syndrome." Unable to speak or move, he painstakingly dictated the realities of living in his frozen body with a still-vital mind by blinking his eye as a physical therapist pointed at a letter board. He wrote his entire memoir that way, letter by letter. The well-chosen details on the page in Bauby's story reflect this method: his words are precise, his memories are lush and exact. No word is wasted in his uncompromising story.

Nearly everyone wants insight into what will happen when they encounter great loss. As writers, we are compelled to put our stories to paper. We fear that grief might wreck us. We want clues about the ways in which we might change, and we want reassurance that when the trouble calms, we will fare well. We also want assurance that the people and places we loved will not be forgotten, because we know that one day we won't be here to speak for them. We want reassurance that our own struggles won't be ignored.

Where will you start your own story of loss? At first the story might seem obvious—it's about what happened. But within that story, with its traditional beginning, middle, and end, there's another story. That story is the personal one, built from those small details in shattered glass that you may not remember right away. Your own story of loss will build connections that may surprise you on the page and in your daily life. And the most surprising part is discovering the story of yourself.

One

DENIAL

THE RIGHT TO WRITE

When you write a memoir about a loss that has affected you, you're telling your story the way you see it. You're the main character, but the story isn't solely about you. Even though grief and loss are uniquely personal, others are involved in the story, perhaps affected by the same loss. Certainly other people have lost a loved one to cancer, been the victim of a crime, lost their job or their home, but your story, even if there are similarities with others, is yours alone. You perceive your loss as world changing, and for you, it is. However, as a writer facing your story of grief for the first time, you may doubt that you have the right to tell that story, especially if you feel it's like one that others have experienced. You might feel that since everyone will have significant loss in their life, what new or different perspective can you bring in your writing? Or you may be ready and eager to write, and even have the story planned thoroughly in your mind, but you worry that your story may hurt a loved one, cause people to think poorly about you, or even offend an authority figure in your life.

Your loss may not have made headlines the way a natural disaster, a war, or even a local crime might have. Your story may have only shaken you, or your family, or your neighborhood. If it did make headlines, you might feel that your perspective is less valuable. The newspapers wrote plenty, you say. What could I contribute? The story of a war, a disaster, or something as tragically common as cancer is so large that perhaps you think that your role in it doesn't matter.

But it does. You experienced a loss, and you want to write about it. At writing conferences and workshops, students have different goals in mind: some want to see their work published, but others would like to share their story only with their families and closest friends. No matter how they envision the outcome, they, like you, sometimes question their right to write. Even if these writers don't acknowledge it yet, they've found the time to attend a conference or workshop because somewhere inside of them pulses the sense that it's time to be among other writers. They're looking for a signal that will indicate for them how to start writing the stories that won't leave them alone. Sharing craft notes at the coffee station, they thumb through the program wishing they could sit in two lectures at once. There's so much to learn, and for many writers beginning memoirs of loss, being in the company of other writers is the first time they truly feel that they're not alone in their desire to write about the grief that has shaped them. Some may worry that writing about their grief could erase the grief itself as well as what they've lost entirely from their lives. For example, author Karen Salyer McElmurray writes in her memoir, *Surrendered Child: A Birth Mother's Journey*, that even though she is a writer, she at first turned away from writing about the loss of her son. In her memoir, she wonders, "If I . . . truly write, will I come to the end of remembering, of grieving, and will there be nothing left?"

Picking up that pen or opening the document on your computer called "memoir" is the first step in no longer denying your right to write.

When Denial Becomes Permission to Write

Elisabeth Kübler-Ross's first stage of grief, "Denial," is the time when the dying, for that is who the book was originally written about, don't yet believe that they are facing death. They may deny that a diagnosis is accurate, or that their lives are coming to an end. They're beginning the process of understanding what is happening to them. If you are writing about losing a loved one, or a beloved time, place, or way of life, you may find that you're in a kind of denial, too, rejecting the notion that you have the ability—or the right—to write about your loss. Denial holds you back from taking that first vital step toward shaping your story into one that you can really understand, that allows to you see not only what happened, but understand how your grief has forged the years that followed.

C. S. Lewis, author of the beloved fantasy series The Chronicles of Narnia, as well as the classic grief memoir written after the death of his wife, *A Grief Observed,* compared the feeling of grief to feeling afraid. Trepidation, or fear, can be useful in beginning to write about grief, because that fear of going backward means that you recognize your desire to be honest.

This chapter will focus on ways that you can encourage yourself to take that first step and give yourself permission to put aside any denial that's holding you back from writing about your grief. You will learn ways to start putting those shattered pieces of memory and fact together to build your memoir's foundation. We will discuss how keeping a journal and writing loose thoughts and images as hot and bright as sparks can illuminate your story. We'll also examine how distance from your sorrow adds perspective to your writing and helps you to look directly and inquisitively at the difficult events that caused your grief.

Writing When You're Ready

Darin Strauss, author of three novels, wrote his memoir, *Half a Life*, more than twenty years after the car accident that is the central story in the memoir. Shortly before his high school graduation, Strauss was driving his father's car when he collided with a classmate on a bicycle. She died as a result of the accident. In his memoir, he tells the story of the accident and his life afterward, as well as his coming to terms with his guilt, sorrow, and growing up. Now that he's an adult, Strauss says that at eighteen, he couldn't have written the book; time had to pass before he was ready. Distance from the event that caused your grief can shed light that's necessary when you're writing about the tough stuff. What caused your grief is in the past, and your perspective has changed naturally as you've continued to survive.

Writing about grief forces you to face yourself. You may have positive and negative feelings about what happened or your role in it, you may feel shame or pride or both. You might literally want to go back to places that at one time you weren't ready to see again. You're doing these things that are both painful and rewarding as you bring back those parts of yourself that you may have thought had been eradicated by loss. Write when you're ready to, Strauss says.

Author Kathryn Rhett, editor of the anthology *Survival Stories: Memoirs of Crisis*, who also wrote about her daughter's birth in the memoir *Near Breathing: A Memoir of a Difficult Birth*, calls the act of writing through grief participation in a fellowship. I call it community. My mother calls it "the club"; one you may not want to belong to, but life experience has awarded you that merit badge.

In her memoir, Rhett writes of her unwilling entry into that fellowship, capturing on paper the moments after she has given birth and learned from her husband that their child is in the ICU. Her own ability to face what will be a touch and go situation (their daughter survives) begins here, with a moment of denial.

> I was bleeding and bleeding, and kept changing the pad, hooking a new one onto the barbaric belt. Women used to have to wear these all the time, I thought, and what did they use before the belt was invented? Rags, I thought, rags, thinking of anything to keep from thinking.

In this excerpt from her memoir, Rhett writes of denial itself, "thinking of anything to keep from thinking" and of focusing on the fragmented and small personal details that are true for her in that moment, and of women throughout time.

Traveling along the road to writing honestly about what happened, you'll feel that you're both moving forward in your life and moving back in time as you look at your loss with a writer's purpose. You're not denying that the fire exists. Instead, you've taken hold of a pen, and with it, extend your hand toward what has already burned you once.

The Writers' Journal

One way to ease into memoir is to develop the journal-keeper's habit of capturing all kinds of raw materials like images, sounds, the sensation of textures, and ideas even when you're not at the keyboard or with pen in hand. Keep yourself in the world of your memoir by daydreaming when you can, and letting your creative mind wander. These raw materials are shards, too, and when you examine them, they add depth and breadth to what you might feel is a story too sad, big, or alternately too limited to write.

"Writing nonfiction," says Pulitzer Prize–nominated author Lee Martin, author of eight books including the memoirs *Such a Life*, *Turning Bones*, and *From Our House*, "begins with curiosity, contradiction, confusion. Then it has somewhere to go."

Whether or not you're someone who has kept journals before, go ahead and start one to accompany this book. No one but you will see it. This journal is where you will sift through the raw material and shattered glass that you will develop into your memoir. Beginning your memoir from a place of change or uncertainty gives you somewhere to start on the page, and lets you pose questions to yourself that your writing can try to answer.

Keeping a journal is where you can begin to explore those questions, including the ways that you've experienced denial, how you will grant yourself permission to revisit your grief and write about it, and what it feels like when your hand is over that personal fire. A journal is a safe place to argue with yourself, explore, question, grieve, and celebrate.

I've kept journals for almost as long as I could write. My very first journal was an inch-thick diary with a flimsy metal lock and key. The green vinyl cover has ONE YEAR DIARY stamped across the face in official-looking gold, a grown-up style that promised a place for serious record-keeping. On the first page, I wrote, "Wednesday, 1969," commemorating the unofficial launch of a writerly frame of mind.

I was a few months into being nine years old. That diary's short entries dip in and out of the minutiae of elementary school: being elected dues treasurer for my Scout troop, seeing The Beatles' movie *Yellow Submarine* (which I deemed "very funny"), and the dullness of a substitute teacher who never seemed to leave. On the surface, these don't seem to be notes for a future memoir, but they are short glimpses into my life as a child innately staking a claim to the everyday moments that helped my life move forward, even as deep grief gripped my home. The journal entries and the need to discover my role in my life are evidence of giving myself permission to write.

My journals mirror my life back to me, so that when I choose to, I can look closely at moments that have passed and start to understand what they mean. Even now, my journals function as a repository for loose ideas. (Of course, sometimes they're merely the closest blank sheet of paper to jot down a grocery list or sketch a quick picture, but these can be material for reflection, too.)

Your journals in their most raw state are for no one's eyes but your own, and they're merely one tool of many in writing your memoir. The journals can be cathartic, but don't mistake them for finished work. They're not intended to be the kind of writing that would engage another reader or do justice to your story. In your journal, catch the moments in life that won't leave you alone but you're not sure why. As you write your memoir, you'll find that it's important to come back often to those moments and examine how they figure into the puzzle that is your ongoing story.

MY STORY:

Since I'm such a devoted keeper of journals, I was stunned to discover a big gap in a journal from the summer of 1992. I was thirty-two. The entry from that Fourth of July is about sitting with friends at a fireworks show and making whistles out of blades of grass. The next entry consists of two undated pages that start with, "Sarah died. This is the first time I have written that down."

The entry after that is dated November 13th—four months later. That entry reads, "I am just waiting for winter to be over." The obituary page from the August 15,

1992, *Boston Globe* and the stub of an airline ticket from Atlanta to Boston are folded into the journal's pages: the only physical remnants of a time of denial, a time before I was ready to write about my searing grief.

On August 13, 1992, my mother called to tell me that Sarah had died. My sister Sarah had been at home, recovering from yet another hospital stay to treat an infection. Her boyfriend found her when he came home from work; she had died during the day, in their bed. He called our mother. When she arrived at Sarah's apartment, just a few miles from her own, the ambulance had already arrived. I remember Mom's phone call, I remember calling the airline, then calling my boss late at night to take an emergency leave from work. I remember one of my closest friends coming over to sit with me until it was time to leave for the airport. And I wrote nothing.

A doctor might say I was experiencing a kind of shock, or that my journal pages from this life-changing time were so stunningly blank because I was in denial. I had known since childhood that Sarah, six years younger than me, lived with an illness that would someday take her life. Her illness was diagnosed when she was a year old, and at the time, she hadn't been expected to live past the age of three. As she grew up, Sarah knew this, too. And yet, when that day came, I couldn't tell the story of the moment that had leapt from the shadows. I couldn't put my grief into words, and didn't go back to my journals for months.

A dozen years later, as I began to write my memoir, those blank pages were stark evidence of how my sister's death disoriented me, first when it happened and then again when I tried to write about it later. I felt lost without the help of my earlier self reporting back from the front lines of the tragedy.

So, when I first tried to write a coherent retelling about my sisters' deaths and how my family changed, I wrote the story as fiction. I conflated two sisters into one, believing that the actual events as I had experienced them would overwhelm my readers and me. But when I started the story that way, it didn't sit right, so I turned them back into two people.

One day I argued with a friend who was critiquing my fiction. "The sisters' names are too similar," she told me. "You'll have to change the names if you want people to follow this story."

I knew when she said that what the real problem was. This wasn't going to work as fiction. It was a memoir: a true story.

"These were real people," I told my friend. "I want their story to be as accurate as possible, and I want to tell the truth about their real lives."

Telling their true story and mine meant that I would have to become brave enough to poke my hand back into an emotional fire that had already burned me badly. I would have to read my journals from that time, even those with gaps, and reexperience that sorrow up close. But in doing so, I knew that I would remember my sisters on the page the most honest and genuine way that I knew how. I gave myself permission to grieve all over again.

Opening Your Eyes and Ears When Your Journal's Not at Hand

When I asked author Abigail Thomas about writing through grief, she told me, "you have to be as honest as you can." Thomas, author of six books, including the highly regarded memoirs *A Three Dog Life: A Memoir* and *Safekeeping: Some True Stories from a*

Life, says that a writer has to figure out what's prodding them about what they want to write. "If you're writing about loss, you've already got the subject," she says, but there are so many ways to approach the very large thing you want to say.

So where do you find your story in the overwhelming topic of loss? "You can't just attack the whole thing," she says. "You have to start with a small memory."

In her memoir, *A Three Dog Life,* which chronicles Thomas's life and marriage after her husband's traumatic brain injury, she writes a short scene about visiting the wool store where she buys her knitting yarn. She arrives there with a pen and paper. In a scene that takes up only about half a page, she establishes the central question of the memoir.

"I'm taking a poll," I say. "What is the one thing that stays stable in your life?"

Thomas asks this question of three people she already knows and a fourth she does not know.

At first glance, the scene is lighthearted and doesn't appear to directly address her loss. The action occurs in a place that's not by definition dramatic: no funeral, no hospital, no accident scene. A woman enters a store where she's a regular customer, carrying a notebook and a deceptively simple question. Instead of tackling her memoir's large subject in one gesture, Thomas writes a scene about a brief interaction that introduces the memoir's theme and brings readers comfortably into her story. Each of the four characters in the store has a different answer to her question. And the author? She doesn't have an answer. She has merely introduced a theme of the book—instability and change.

Focusing on a life-changing injury and the changes it brings necessarily turns you away from the normal, comfortable parts of your life. A visit to a store where you shop regularly? Less so. Life, even in grief, is not "all huge thoughts and ghastly moments," Thomas says. "It's hilarious and beautiful, and for me, that's my material."

When I was writing early drafts of my memoir, I was driving to work, bored with the programming on my usual radio station. I scanned the stations to find something else to listen to in morning traffic. My dial jumped past a classic rock station and stayed there just long enough for me to hear the opening notes of a twenty-year-old hit that Sarah and I had sung together, making up new words and screaming into our fists like pretend microphones. I stopped on that station and sang along. Our parody lyrics came to me in an instant, and I laughed and cried, delighted to be hollering "two tickets for rats and mice" again in our old imitation of a nineteen-seventies Eddie Money song, and mournful and angry that I was singing it alone.

I didn't realize until later that day that I had begun writing a scene that would appear in the final version of the book. I hadn't been writing, I had been driving to work.

Why a Brain-Spark Is like Turning on a Light

You might not yet know where your memoir starts and ends, who's really the good guy or the bad guy, or even what the heart of the story truly is until you've written enough down to start figuring that out. These are elements of plot and character, and they are the heart and soul of your story.

But before there's plot or character, there's the brain-spark. In a brain-spark, put on the page whatever images and words are on your mind. Once you do that, you can shine a light on those details and memories. Not all the raw stuff will end up in your memoir, and probably none of it in its raw state. I can't give you a timeline for how long this will take. It might happen as you construct your plot. The more you write, the more you start to remember, which leads to seeing new ways that pieces of your story can fit together.

"Where do I start?" a woman asked me when she learned

that I taught writing. She had a memoir in her that she "just had to write," but she was anxious about how to take the first step.

Just start writing, I told her. Don't worry about how the material will come together, or if what you write is any good. Just get it out of your brain and onto the page. Organization— the plot—will come later. That organization will be the memoir's narrative arc: the beginning, middle, and end that describe your story back to you.

Katharine Weber, author of six books, including the memoir *The Memory of All That: George Gershwin, Kay Swift, and My Family's Legacy of Infidelities,* about growing up with her distant mother, unreliable father, and the impact of dishonesty, suggests that one way to start is to imagine how you would tell your story to a good friend. Weber calls the brain-spark a rough first draft, which she compares to a film's unedited footage, or the dailies. These are the raw materials from which you'll make plot and character choices.

That getting-it-onto-the-next-page phase is the first step, agrees Ethan Gilsdorf, whose memoir *Fantasy Freaks and Gaming Geeks* examines his lifelong fascination with gaming and fantasy. While his original intent was to write a memoir about his relationship with his mother after she suffered a disabling brain aneurysm when he was just twelve, he found that he wasn't sure how to write that book, or if he could. As a journalist, he sought assignments about *The Lord of the Rings,* J. R. R. Tolkien, and "that kind of thing," he says. As he wrote those articles and more, he started to see how his fascination with games like Dungeons & Dragons intersected with the escapism he sought as a teenage boy whose mother had become a creature he called "The Momster."

Getting it onto the page helps figure out the ultimate heart of the story. "With trauma and grief," Gilsdorf explains, "you might have a vague sense that you weren't given the chance to succeed," or in his case, that "my mother died when I was young but I'm not sure what the effect was. The real understanding happens on the page." In writing, even in that get-it-on-the-page stage, you learn to see your life differently. As a young man, Gilsdorf told himself that his mother's illness had made him strong and independent. In writing the memoir, he came to realize that he had never properly mourned the loss of his mother.

Writing to Find Out

"I don't know yet" was my sister Sarah's de facto motto. She didn't know when a set of lab tests would come back or what new information they might show. The unpredictable nature of her illness kept her from ever being sure she could attend a class, go to a movie with friends, or if a minor discomfort meant something greater. In a larger sense, our whole family didn't know yet what would happen to any of us. Write whatever you like in those early brain-spark sessions, and as you do, remind yourself that you don't know yet what shape your story will take.

> **TIP: Perhaps no one asked you or encouraged you to tell your story. Go ahead now and give yourself permission: invite yourself to tell your story. Just as there is no "right" way to grieve, there is no "right" way to remember. Your memories are your own. Writing your story is just that—*your* story.**

If your story matters to you, then that's more than enough reason to write. Writing from your perspective is your privilege. Writing through your grief and loss allows you to claim the way the things happened for you. If you write with honesty and attention to character, imagery, plot, and theme, your memoir will resonate with your family, your friends, and if you choose to write for a wider readership, your story will matter to people you don't yet know.

Claiming What's True for You

Early in the process of writing my memoir about my sisters, our mother gave me a box of Sarah's journals, calendars, and school notebooks. Mom wanted me to have all the material I might need to tell our family's story. I had lost my two sisters, and she had lost her two youngest daughters. Our stories were similar, but they were profoundly different.

"I have Sarah's writing," Mom told me. My husband helped her carry in a battered cardboard crate. The box was piled high with folders and notebooks. Although my mother is traditionally organized down to the last file folder and rubber band, this box wasn't labeled with her usual black marker pen and taped-on index cards. The box wasn't labeled at all.

The crate lurked on the floor of my writing room for more than a month while I debated with myself. I wasn't sure that I had the right to read the contents or if I even wanted to. Sarah's diaries, yearbooks, creative writing assignments from high school, her entrance essay for college, and submissions for a writing workshop she was ultimately too sick to attend would have put me in close touch with her most intimate thoughts. Her words would tell me in her voice exactly what had been on her mind and in her heart.

I couldn't deny that I had the rare opportunity to see into my beloved sister's heart and mind. She was no longer here to answer my questions in person, and I missed her terribly. Maybe the answers would be on those pages, in her deliberate, rounded, cursive handwriting, but I couldn't shake the mental image of my little sister not-so-playfully slapping my hand and laughing, telling me, "that's private!" She wouldn't have let me read her diaries if she were alive.

Ultimately, I read her death certificate and a few writing-class essays, knowing that those items had already been seen by others: the death certificate by the Suffolk County, Massachusetts, medical examiner, the essays by writing teachers and classmates. But I chose to respect Sarah's personal diaries by not reading them. I put the box in my attic, because the story I wanted to write was the story of the sister who survived. That is my story. My sisters' lives and deaths are central to who I am. Their illnesses and deaths shaped our family, and that was what shaped my memoir's plot.

Permission to write meant not reading Sarah's diaries, and not pretending to see the world through Susie's eyes. Permission meant agreeing with myself that this would be my story, told the way I saw it.

How Stories Cast a Spell

Stories existed before writing. For example, the famous cave paintings in Lascaux, France, are more than seventeen thousand years old. More than one hundred paintings in browns, blacks, and greens made from minerals depict massive horses, bison, lions, and other animals. Experts believe that these illustrations show hunting successes or celebrate ritual. They are stories without words.

Fairy tales, which tend to be pretty gruesome, usually begin with the phrase "once upon a time." This simple introductory clause has become a spell, an incantation to the modern child falling asleep to the sound of a loved one reading his favorite tale. A story is about to start, an account of vanquished troubles.

Writing through grief invites you to write evocatively and honestly about an emotional, physical, or cultural blow that has irrevocably changed your life. As you write, you create a story that examines that grief and what surrounds it. As you write, you forge a coherent account of your loss that connects even the smallest, broken details with the blunt force of emotion and the recognition that you have survived to do many things, including write your true story.

Instead of denying yourself the right to write, grant yourself permission to pick up the pen, open the notebook, or create
a new file on your computer. Stories are the oldest method of
recording ourselves as we change. Humans have always done
this. Let's begin again, with your story.

THE NEXT STEP

1. Dedicate a journal to the exercises in this book. Your
   journal can be any collection of blank pages you like,
   including digital ones. Be prepared to use this journal
   and subsequent ones to expand the exercises as you
   choose. You can also draw in a journal, doodle, weep,
   laugh, spill your coffee, or even figuratively gnash your
   teeth. Writing about grief requires honesty, guts, and
   creativity. No one will see these pages but you.

2. Give yourself formal permission to write about your
   grief by making a pledge to the person, people, relationship, or place missing from your life. You might want to
   decorate a sheet of paper, draft a contract, or simply
   print this out and keep it handy.

   > I pledge to you, (X) that my intentions in writing
   > about my grief are good. I want to write honestly
   > about losing (X) so that I will feel (X) and be able to
   > (X) in the future.
   >
   > Signed _____.

3. Write about a time when you did not tell the truth about
   your experience with grief. Where were you? How old
   were you? How recent was the loss? Who or what were
   you grieving? Who asked you about it, and why? What
   did you say to them?
   a. Write this exercise in the first-person point of view,
      beginning with this phrase: "I didn't tell (name of other
      person) about my grief because. . . ."

b. Be as specific in detail as you can, but don't stop to wrack your memory, just go with what you know for right now. The loss you write about in this exercise can be anything that was or continues to be significant to you.

4. Write about a time when you and another person involved in the same grief-causing event realized that you had different impressions or beliefs about what happened or why. Make a list of the facts that you know about that event. Make a second list of your memories about that event. If you are comfortable doing so, share your list with that other person. (They don't need to make their own list unless they want to try this exercise themselves.) How do your memories differ or how do you think they might differ? How are they similar?

5. Complete these six statements directed toward the person, place, or thing that you have lost. If these trigger more ideas, keep going. What points of entry into your story do they inspire?

Since you've been gone, I have . . .	
I still keep . . .	
I won't tell anyone about . . .	
A funny thing that happened with you (or when I lived there) was that time when . . .	
Where did the . . .	
You would be happy to know . . .	

6. Why does writing about grief matter to you? Check the boxes and add a sentence or two that will help you focus your goals.

I want my grief memoir to tell my family's story.	
I want my grief memoir to tell my story within that family.	
I want my grief memoir to recount a time in history that's faded or not remembered by others the way I remember.	
I want my experience as (X) to be honored.	
I want readers to understand what it is/was really like to (X).	

7. Denying yourself the right to examine your whole story leaves you with only the partial story. Try writing a passage or two about a character or an event in your story that you've hesitated to put on paper because you worry that what you write will offend or hurt someone. When you're satisfied with what you've written, ask yourself if it's as damaging as you had feared. If it is, what would make you comfortable with the material so that you can use it in your memoir? You may also choose never to use it, and find that simply writing it down has cleared the air.

Two

ANGER

∾

WRITING THE WORST AND BEST IN CHARACTERS (INCLUDING YOURSELF) AND WHY THERE'S NO PLOT WITHOUT CONFLICT

Writing our stories of loss, we often find that we're angry, wanting to shout "why me?" as we recall our vanished lives or homes or broken families. If we are the villain—in any way—we want to make things right, even if that's no longer entirely possible. On the page and in our lives, we insist, relentlessly, that what has happened is unfair. We resent the occurrence of a tragedy in our lives, and rage against undeserved fate.

In the Kübler-Ross structure, the second stage of grief is "Anger." A person facing death might search for someone or something to blame for what's happening to them, or be resentful of those who aren't yet dying. As you write your memoir, you might find that you're angry at the action, person, or even the slippery unknown that caused your loss and the changes that followed. You may be angry at an individual who didn't behave the way you believe they should have, or angry at something you can't see and may not be able to name, like an abnormal cell in a body or a political upheaval. What in your experience with grief angers you? For a writer, that anger can be an aspect of plot, because a well-structured plot moves forward when a change occurs that forces the characters— including you—to react.

In this chapter, we will examine what makes a character the "good guy" or the "bad guy," and why those two labels aren't always immediately apparent in stories of grief. We will examine how you as a writer can trace the elements in your own story that changed, discovering how moments you may have overlooked can be pivotal in your writing. We'll look at examples and exercises that you can apply to your memoir, clarifying how to write about that anger and change in a way that's interesting, true, and leads to renewal for you as a writer and as the character on the page.

Be as angry as you like in the pages of your journal and in your brain-spark drafts. That's where raw anger belongs. There's a big difference between writing in a journal (or talking to your therapist) and writing to be read. If your intention in writing about your loss is to point fingers, you'll do a disservice to your memoir and to yourself. Vindictiveness diminishes the quality of the writing. To regain your balance, try looking at an incident of anger from two sides. Maybe you're writing about your divorce. What did you see in your ex when you married? There must have been something. Maybe, I tell my students if they're stumped, your ex was really good at parallel parking. That's something.

Margaux Fragoso, in *Tiger, Tiger: A Memoir*, writes about her anger at Peter Curran, a pedophile with whom she had a fifteen-year relationship that began when she was seven and he was fifty-one. The memoir is candid, unsettling, and angry. However, she handles the story with compassion for him and for herself as a child and young woman. Jeanette Walls writes in her bestselling memoir *The Glass Castle* about her parents' increasing homelessness, alcoholism, and irresponsibility to their children, but she tells the story with remarkable insight and love. In *The Liars' Club,* her memoir of her childhood in a small Texas town, author Mary Karr shows us her volatile mother and her pugilistic, alcoholic father in such a way that we like them in spite of ourselves. By showing the potential for good that was lost or squandered, these authors let a reader feel the loss even more poignantly.

As a grieving person, you may be angry that a parent, a doctor, an employer, or a partner was instrumental in creating the experience that brought about your grief. You might be ashamed that you're angry at someone who has died and left you to live without them. Because you're a writer, put that anger to work on the page in the service of your story.

> **TIP: You've been wronged by your loss, but you know that grief and grievance aren't the same thing. Author Katharine Weber believes that grievance "keeps you in one place" and doesn't give you, as a writer, the freedom to resolve how you feel about your story and re-create it well on the page. Staying in one place is also antithetical to plot. A plot requires that the main character change in some way, and there can be no change if everything stays the same. A writer exploring grief can be thoughtful, curious, and even generous. And, as a character, he or she has to change by the end of her story.**

Be Generous to Your Characters, No Matter Who They Are

You are a character in your memoir. In fact, you're the protagonist. As a character, you're composed of many facets that come into play in your daily life. For example, I'm a daughter and a wife. I'm not a mother, by choice, but I'm a teacher. I'm sentimental about every pet I've ever had, but I can get impatient in crowds of people. Like all real human beings, these traits make me complicated in real life and on the page.

In his memoir *In the Sanctuary of Outcasts,* Neil White writes about the eighteen months he spent in federal prison for bank fraud. White served his time at a facility in Carville, Louisiana, that not only housed inmates, but was also the last functioning leprosarium in the United States. White had reason to be angry, not only at the bureaucratic decision that sent him to a prison that caused him at first to fear for his health (until he learned that nearly all humans are resistant to Hansen's Disease, or leprosy, which is treatable) but angry at himself, for his illegal attempts to maintain a lifestyle that ultimately sent him to jail. And yet, he is generous to himself and his characters as he writes about his family, other prisoners, patients, and guards, and his own role in the story.

He writes with a clear eye about the man he was before he went to prison. That earlier Neil was a man who made serious mistakes that took him from his two children and his wife. But he's also a man with whom we can empathize.

Ruminating on how this situation charged with anger changed him, White told me that before prison, "all I cared about was maintaining a façade of perfection." But what are the odds, he wonders, "of a guy obsessed with his own image going to the one place in America where outward image meant nothing?"

In Carville, one of the luxuries to which White no longer had access was cologne. He writes:

I missed my cologne. . . . I hated to walk into the visiting room . . . without my fragrance. In prison, cologne was contraband.

But one of his regular tasks was to help in the prison library, and White, unable to accept how his life has changed, does something both foolish and forlorn.

As I organized the periodicals and flipped through the pages, I tore out the aromatic inserts. I stockpiled the samples in my locker, and before visiting hours, I opened the strips and rubbed them against my shirt until the fragrance permeated my green uniform.

Later in the paragraph, White jokes about being the best-smelling inmate there, but his careful descriptions and use of words and phrases that imply restriction, like "stockpiled" and "green uniform," belies the gentle joke. The reader can have compassion for his desire to bring one of the comforts of his prior life to the blunt reality of prison.

White says that writing about this after the fact allowed him to see himself as a character with both positive and negative traits. "It's easier now to laugh about my hoarding scent strips to smell good in prison," he says. "We can never be entirely objective about ourselves, but if you don't have some objectivity, you're not going to be credible."

In his memoir, *Fantasy Freaks and Gaming Geeks*, Ethan Gilsdorf writes honestly about what it was like to be twelve years old and angry toward his recently disabled mother, who had suffered a brain aneurysm that left her unable to drive, cook, or look after her three children. Here, he watches her on the stairs.

Go ahead, fall, I find myself thinking.
"Be careful, Mom," I say, my tone full of false concern, barely masking my annoyance.

Gilsdorf is brutally honest here about his own self-involvement as a young teenager, but what twelve-year-old doesn't have powerful moments of selfishness?

"[That] was a tough place to go" on the page, Gilsdorf says. "But ultimately, the reader appreciates the author portraying himself as not one hundred percent blameless."

TIP: What can you write about yourself honestly and objectively that shows you not only in your best light, but in your worst light, and therefore, most truthful? Are you a romantic partner to someone? A widow or widower? A parent? A working professional or a retiree? How do these terms define you to yourself and to others? Do you chafe against any of these roles, and if so, why?

MY STORY:

When I felt comfortable enough with a friend or colleague to allow myself to tell them what had happened to my family—that both of my younger sisters died, one as a child, the other as a young woman, that my once-gentle father lost his bearings and for a while, his mind, becoming explosive and unreliable, and that our family broke up, the listeners almost always asked me how I made it through. They truly wanted to know. My guess is that they were wondering about themselves and what they could handle if they had to, or were counting up the ways in which they had already proved to themselves that they were able to make it through their own tragedies.

Before you write about your grief, you may not know how you made it through. Writing your memoir is the way you pursue that trail of how and why. Revisiting certain moments in your life in order to write about them may make you angry, or remind you of blame, guilt, misunderstanding, and sorrow. You might resent having to "go there" again after you've quashed those feelings. But your desire to write about your loss is a crucial part of your story. You're willing to experience your difficult emotions again in order to write well about how you felt at one time and may still feel. Your anger may also be what brings you to the page.

In 1969, after my sister Susie died, our mother dumped the leftover Methotrexate, an anticancer drug, into the toilet in our yellow and white bathroom, sending flotillas of the tablets into the swirling water. She told me this much later, when I was a grown woman. Even after more than forty years her anger was still strong: she slapped the table when she spoke, making our coffee cups jump. Then and now, her anger at Susie's leukemia and at her own impotence in easing her daughter's misery is very real.

My anger is a few geometric degrees away from hers, but it's strong in its own way. She is the mother, and I'm the daughter and sister. I'm angry still that our mother was in emotional pain. I remember watching her cleaning out the bathroom cabinet and crying, and the abrupt way she closed the bathroom door so I wouldn't see. She wanted and needed to be alone, and not share that grief with ten-year-old me. In my imagination, I see my mother, in her early thirties, crying in the Jack and Jill bathroom that connected Sarah's bedroom to the one Susie and I shared. In my imagination, I can see her methodically opening one after another of the prescription bottles that she took from the shelves and dumping them into the toilet, the same one where she sat with the lid down and brushed my hair, the same bathroom with a stepstool for Sarah to reach the sink and clean her teeth. I imagine that the single window is open and the thin white curtains are blowing, although it would have been November. I remember the harsh light in the room, the bath toys on the edge of the big tub that fit two little girls at once, the super-sized Johnson's Baby Shampoo and the stick-on flowers that kept us from skidding on the floor of the tub.

She knows that she should have returned the unused medication to the hospital or to our pharmacist, but the toilet is where they belonged, she said. Putting unused medication in the toilet, unwilling to be forgiving of her daughter's death even years later, might make her a flawed character in some people's eyes. But depicting her honestly makes her complicated and real, and makes the scene vivid and memorable.

Anger and Your Memoir's Health

Because anger can be scorching when we grieve, descriptions and scenes written in anger can capture the crackle and spark of rage. Lively writing is often compelling writing. And the adrenaline that comes with anger is often the push you need in writing about difficult subjects to get to the page and stay there until a draft of a scene or even a chapter, if you're lucky, is done.

But for all of its potential value in helping you bring strong work to the page, anger can also be dangerous to the health of your memoir. A story told entirely in anger isn't interesting; it's a one-sided tale of woe and blame. That author has merely pointed fingers. She may have made herself feel better momentarily, but she has not engaged her readers or been fair to her characters or herself.

To confound the matter, antagonists are not always people. Sometimes they're intangible forces, like an illness, a drug or alcohol addiction, or environmental devastation. Sometimes illness just happens. Accidents are called that for a reason. If your grief was caused, even in part, by environmental devastation, how far back in the causal chain do you want to go, and would that derail your narrative? (After a certain point, probably.)

For me, this focus is one of the places where real writing skill kicks in. Since you can't easily describe the physical characteristics of something that has no actual body, and you certainly can't easily understand what motivates a nonhuman antagonist, how do you write effectively about that destructive force?

In *A Portrait of the Artist as a Young Man,* no less an author than James Joyce writes about the "whatness of a thing." I love this odd, surprisingly intricate phrase that he uses in writing the way his character Stephen Dedalus explains the act of seeing. Joyce uses the word "luminous" too—a characteristic you might not immediately ascribe to an antagonistic force, but isn't it a kind of glow, even one you might call malevolent, that makes your antagonist unforgettable?

TIP: As you brain-spark and develop your plot, try to expand on the elements that make your otherwise nonphysical antagonist a physical thing. What did the wounds on your loved one's skin look like, and how did you feel the first time you bandaged them? What washed up on your hometown beach, and how did the volunteers console each other when they could no longer rescue the damaged wildlife? Can you learn what happened in that Petri dish, that airplane, that executive committee meeting? If you really want to reach for luminance, what can you write about this nebulous antagonist that's oddly and surprisingly memorable? For example, in *The Year of Magical Thinking,* Joan Didion doesn't write about her daughter Quintana's beauty as she lies unconscious in an intensive care unit, but of her swollen face and matted hair. Didion is, as always, painfully honest, and it's in the shock of reading her unadorned writing that we feel her sorrow.

An elegant sentence about a loathed or hurtful antagonistic force can bring what's made you angry into sharp focus for you and for your reader. As a writer, you've allowed that antagonist real power in your story, leaving no question for the reader about the depth or ferocity of your grief.

One last note on the subject of writing characters. Just because someone you love is sick, dead, or has become atypical in some way, that doesn't necessarily beatify them. In fact, an author shortchanges a loved one if that person or place is depicted as being too perfect. They become one-dimensional, unbelievable, and even though it's the last thing you'd ever want, they become just a little bit unlikeable.

My sister Sarah ate with her mouth open, and smacked her lips. I hate that. The sound of lip-smacking at the table (or anywhere else) makes my flesh crawl more than the screech of fingernails on a blackboard. It's taken me until now to realize that Sarah probably ate this way because when she was a baby her medication caused mouth ulcers. She must have learned to eat solid food at a time when her mouth was painfully sensitive. Nevertheless, we spent half our childhoods with me shouting, "stop smacking" at the table, and her ignoring me, smacking and popping away

These are not perfect sisters. One's irritated—me—and the other is irritating—Sarah. These are real sisters, acting real.

So, Who's Really the Good Guy?

Only the most simplistic stories have a clear-cut "bad guy" and "good guy." In the Western films of the nineteen fifties and sixties, you could tell pretty quickly who was who. The bad guy wore a black hat. He was usually unshaven, was often vaguely "ethnic," which in that era of Hollywood implied "dangerous." He generally appeared to be down on his luck.

The good guy wore the white hat and the clean, courageous countenance. He smiled a lot, and had a virtuous woman at his side. We knew that the good guy and bad guy would fight it out, and when their shoot-out scene arrived, we knew who would prevail. The good guy was the protagonist, and the bad guy was the antagonist. The hero versus the villain.

You are the protagonist in your memoir, and I'm the protagonist in mine. And that memoir includes an array of my relevant faults. I consumed illegal drugs by the pocketful. I was hurtful to my parents and my sisters. I stole items of greater value than I wrote about in my memoir, and sometimes even in my journals. In retrospect, I was a pretty typical 1970s "troubled teen."

As you write about yourself, work to capture who you were "then," whatever "then" means for your story. In this chapter, character-exploration exercises will help you see yourself as protagonist and others as antagonist. If you still have journals from earlier times in your life, reading them can provide some of this insight. So can freewrites, or listening to music from the period of time your memoir covers, reading newspapers and magazines from the era for the headlines, the ads, and the prices. What triggers a memory? Quick, grab a pen or get to the keyboard and brain-spark, and be honest with yourself. A scene will come later.

We know firsthand that stories of grief and loss are not simple. Our primary character—who some might call the hero— prevails in some ways, but loses greatly in others. Our antagonist—who some might call the villain—may have simply been a person in the wrong place at the wrong time, an inchoate force, or even someone who puts his foot in his mouth and says the exact wrong thing.

MY STORY:

After Sarah died, I took a month's leave from my job. I wanted to be near our mother for her sake and for mine. She and my father were divorced and didn't have a friendly relationship, and I was now the only surviving child. I wasn't emotionally ready to return to work and face questions about where I'd gone and why, and I didn't want Mom to be alone in her sorrow.

When I did come back, my colleagues were gracious and kind, and I eased back into my job without much trouble, until the chance phone call from an associate who asked where I'd been for so long.

"My little sister died," I told him.

"Wow," he answered. "I know how you feel. I had a hamster die once."

What he said was clumsy, and it made me want to scream at him just when I thought I could make it through a workday without my emotions sidelining me. Extricating myself from the conversation, I simply hung up. At the time, I was angry and hurt. Twenty years later, while I still believe that he stuck his foot squarely in his mouth and was insensitive to my grief, I know that he hadn't known what to say. My loss frightened him. Writing the "good guy" and the "bad guy" in grief memoirs means walking a long mile in the other guy's shoes as well as your own.

A Little Bit Good and a Little Bit Bad

Just as flesh and blood humans are multilayered, no well-written characters are entirely good or entirely bad. When I talk about this concept in a classroom, I ask my students to challenge the notion.

"The Devil," someone invariably offers. "But he was a fallen angel," someone else points out. If he's played in a movie by a dapper actor, I add, he always seems to have impeccable taste in suits. These aren't perfect qualities, but they do give the Devil some depth.

> TIP: As you develop your "bad" characters, try to figure out what made them behave in the way that they did. A doctor may alienate a patient or family member by speaking only in medical jargon or having an abrupt bedside manner. Does that make her a bad person, or is she a person who is uncomfortable when faced with someone else's anxiety?

Is she in some ways unskilled? Perhaps the guy on the phone at my job thought a hamster and a sister held a shared place in the pantheon of loss. Perhaps for him they did. Another example might be the father who strikes his child and establishes Draconian rules in his home. When that child grows up to be a man, he realizes that his father had invested himself in hiding a family secret, and the stress made him rule with a heavy hand.

Your Plot's Probably Not What You Think It Is

Readers find their way into your story not only by recognizing themselves in your characters, but by following the plot. Plot is *the* ubiquitous tool for shaping a story. It's like one of those camping knives that can do anything depending on how you apply it. The slippery thing about plot when writing true stories of grief is that we think, oh, the plot will be easy. It's so obvious to us. There I was, living my regular life, and this terrible thing happened. If you've tried to write that story already and recognized that it's not quite working, you have probably started to sense that a memoir of grief has to be more than just retelling what happened and expecting readers to feel the same sorrow that you feel.

In writing your memoir, the terrible thing that happened is only the *catalyst* for the story. Writers crafting well-told stories of grief face a unique narrative challenge. Stories of loss are not simple. While they have a beginning, middle, and end, the end of the story doesn't suddenly reveal what's caused the grief. Often, it's that particular loss that sets the story in motion, which makes the occurrence of loss the beginning of the plot.

Essayist, poet, and writing teacher Rebecca McClanahan proposes that in writing about loss, the catalyst for telling the story is a moment called "the occasion of the telling." Something in your life now has created in you the urge, even the need, to tell your story.

The real story is not only what happened, but the deeper meaning to the author as she experienced it then and as she looks back on the experience in order to write about it now. The topic of your memoir's deeper meaning can be expressed through those small, shattered-glass details that pull your focus and the reader's focus into the scene itself, rather than confound you as you try to conquer the unwieldy, abstract topic of grief itself head-on. For example, Jo Ann Beard writes of watching the stars through an amber necklace given to her by a friend whose murder is one of the subjects of her essay, "The Fourth State of Matter" in her memoir-in-essays, *The Boys of My Youth*. Kelle Groom, in *I Wore the Ocean in the Shape of a Girl*, writes of looking up the ages at which babies learn to walk, run, and begin to speak. It's in small, heartbreaking details like these that she conveys her own grief in losing her son Tommy, first through giving him up for adoption to family members, and then through his death at fourteen months from leukemia.

> **TIP:** An important early step as you write about your loss is to define for yourself the reason you've decided to write your story now. You've given yourself the permission to write, and have met, for the first or the hundredth time, the anger toward your loss or the difficulty you've had in the grief itself and in framing that grief in a coherent story. The next time you sit down to write, try to identify the catalyst or incident that made you decide to write a memoir.
>
> Taking this a step further, is your "beginning" the chronological start of the story, before a character is born, a war begins, or an accident happens, or is your beginning the occasion of the telling, when something in the present day makes you look back? Prepare to be surprised by what you discover.

The main architect of plot in Western Civilization was Aristotle, the Greek philosopher. In his work *Poetics*, written circa 330 BCE, he made the case for orderly structure in drama. It's also been said that there are only two archetypal plots: a stranger comes to town, or someone takes a journey. Either of these could be, in broad terms, about grief. (What is that "stranger" but illness, the dissolution of a romance, or the tree that fell on your house, or what is that "journey" but your learning to live well after a tragedy?)

Loss creates some of the most irrevocable change there is, and it's change that creates the way a plot moves forward. We grieve things and people and a life that can never be the same. From a writer's perspective, that's conflict. The protagonist wants her old life back, and the antagonist—an illness, a divorce, a war, a lost job—prevents her from ever having that exact life again. How will the protagonist come to terms with the change that's been forced upon her? You turn the page, and start to find out.

The Two Levels of Your Plot

If you take a close look, you'll see that your memoir is about much more than the unfolding of the events that made your grief. A grief story—and any well-written memoir that works to evaluate the effects of an important subject—operates on two levels. The level that's immediately evident is the nominal level, the surface. That's the basic story line. This thing happened, then the other thing, and this other thing.

The substantive level is what runs beneath the story line. Writers of grief memoir strive on the page to understand what their loss means and how it has changed the way they inhabit the world. This is deep stuff, and it's often in the substantive writing that the memoirist does most of her real work.

The substantive part can be found in your nominal writing. For example, a student of mine was dissatisfied with his writing. Every time he sat down to write about a stressful time in his romantic relationship, he became irritated with himself for habitually writing and speaking about the impasse in clipped military jargon. When we talked about why this might be happening, I wondered aloud if he thought that his recent combat experience in Iraq was playing a part in why he was writing in a short, radio-speak style.

"Copy that," he responded automatically, and we laughed. I suggested that he continue to write in the style that was coming naturally and see where it led him. Acknowledging the way in which he expressed his anger helped him consider what he wasn't seeing yet as a writer, and led him toward the substantive level of the piece he was working on. The nominal story was a straightforward account of a difference of opinion between this student and his girlfriend. The substantive story had more to do with how he, as an individual, had learned to deflect conflict.

My student tried to tease me about being his "shrink," but I pointed out to him that some aspects of who he is—in this case, a combat veteran—shape the way he reacts to the world, both in real life and on the page. In the finished piece, the military phrases, abrupt sentences, and even the way he holds his feelings in check through his silences would tell a great deal about the ways his emotions were inaccessible to him.

Your Mixed Emotions Are Part of Your Story

You revisit strong emotions and fears as you write about sadness and loss, and if you're writing accurately and honestly, you may have to revisit places in your mind and in your physical life that disturb you. This is all the more reason to first write in the order that feels most comfortable to you. Emotions don't appear in neat order, which can frustrate you if you feel it's necessary to come to a single, clear emotional perspective on the page. Your mixed emotions are themselves a part of the story you're shaping. Even when emotions feel contradictory—for example, a

deep sadness alongside the happiness that comes from a particular memory—a writer should let the "entire field of emotion in,"
author Rebecca McClanahan recommends. She explained to me
that, "in all good writing that has emotion in it, there's not [just]
a single emotion occurring on the page." One example might be
a description of the conflicting feelings during a floundering
romance, hating someone while having the strong urge to kiss
them.

Nick Flynn feels that a red flag should go up when a writer
finds himself telling a reader how to feel at a particular moment. He's more interested in what he calls "uneasy emotion,"
the awkward or complicated emotional response that forces the
author to confront their inner lives. In this example from Flynn's
memoir *Another Bullshit Night in Suck City,* the author's emotions
toward his father are indeed complicated; he imagines them pub-
licly, forcibly reunited, his own story and appearance reduced,
and a startling, even treacherous statement at the end.

> If I could distill those years into a television game show
> I'd call it *The Apologist.* Today's show: "Fathers Left Out-
> side to Rot" And there I'd sit in an ill-fitting suit, one of
> three or four contestants, looking contrite or defiant or
> inscrutable under the life-draining lights. At some point,
> after I tell an abridged version of my story, the host will
> parade my father out, and we will have a reunion of sorts,
> on national tv, as the camera pans the reactions of the stu-
> dio audience. Before we go a commercial break a caption
> will appear under my face—*He wished his father dead.*

Flynn shows in this excerpt how varied emotions create
conflict. The other contestants in the scene demonstrate contri-
tion, defiance, or inscrutability, but it's the character of Flynn in
this paragraph who both invites and demonstrates mixed emotions. He is forced into what we (and the imaginary television
viewers in the scene) hope will be a happy reunion, but his
concluding sentence makes the opposite very clear. These are

emotions in conflict with each other. And conflict, as you know, drives plot.

Take the Long Way Home

Most writers I know don't actually write in order of beginning, middle, and end. That comes later, after the scenes that make up the story are in draft form, and the scenes that don't belong in the story are put aside.

My creative mind is most productive when I acknowledge that my creative thoughts tend to appear when I allow my mind to drift. I keep a notebook and a pen in my purse, and another in my car. I want to be able to capture a fleeting image before it's gone, if it's a daydream that I think belongs in a essay that I'm writing, or a quick pencil sketch of how to sign the word "vampire" in American Sign Language. (A student taught me: form your first and second fingers into a V-shaped claw and stab your neck while you grimace.)

When I sit at my computer later to write, I can start shaping those ideas into scenes. You might feel thwarted if you try to write the first draft of your memoir in the order that you believe should ultimately take place. Finding that all-important time to write and then getting angry at yourself and your expectations because you can't envision what you think should be the "next" scene is discouraging. If you do this enough, you'll be tempted to give up. What would that be but another loss?

Try to write something every day, no matter what it is. Keep a notebook in the car for those times when you're waiting in the carpool line. Write on an airplane flight instead of trying to nap or watch the movie, or use your lunch break at work for a writing session. For example, I have regular teaching commitments and a variety of other responsibilities and pleasures that vie for my attention, so when I do get to my desk and close the door to my very small writing room, my writing time is limited and valuable. Perhaps today the scene that logically comes next in a piece I'm working on isn't the most vibrant image in my mind or my heart. I've been thinking more about a scene that I feel will come later in the memoir, or in something else entirely. I can imagine the dialogue—or some of it—and have what feel like perfect descriptions of the weather, the characters' facial expressions, and an almost tangible sense of the deeper meaning of their interactions.

Writing is a commitment, Abigail Thomas says. When I asked her about how writers can confront tough subjects, she suggested paying attention to what keeps recurring in your writing, and notice what "echoes" with you. "It takes a lot of guts," she adds. It takes guts to keep that story going, even in bits and pieces as you grab time to write.

A kid telling a story on the playground knows she's got her audience's attention when another kid asks, spellbound, "and then what happened?" Ask yourself that same question, and don't look away. Examine your memories and descriptions for what they really represent in your story. What you find will lead you through.

"This shadow life that could have been ours went flying by," says Lee Martin. "I had to tell the story to myself so that I could understand it more fully." Martin's father, Roy, lost both hands in a tractor accident the year Lee was born. In his memoir, *From Our House,* Martin writes of his father's rage, his mother's grace, and his own relationship with a father hardened by tragedy. Martin is a gifted writing teacher who writes both fiction and nonfiction, and he began the story of his family as a series of essays. The larger, connected plot became clear to him over time. He told me, "I saw that I had a narrative arc: his accident, and our path toward some sort of peace with that."

Martin parallels the shattered glass idea when he observes that, "the material itself is too big. You've got to find one thing to write about, and that unleashes your subconscious." Finding that one thing to write about is your way in to your wider story, no matter what order it comes in.

MY STORY:

After Sarah died, my mother undertook the heartbreaking requirements of canceling Sarah's credit cards, changing the rental agreement for her apartment, and making the necessary changes to all the paperwork that makes up a life. She told me that when she spoke to the social security office about canceling Sarah's disability payments, the clerk asked Sarah's age at death.

"Twenty-seven," Mom told her.

"That's not possible," the clerk said, without empathy. "Check again—that's too young."

Even though a social security office is likely to be accustomed to dealing with young people's deaths, this clerk was insensitive about what she was being told, and so she challenged and inadvertently hurt my mother. And then what happened? My mother told her that it was indeed possible, and offered to send her a copy of the death certificate. Her grief and honesty forced the clerk to adjust her brittle outlook on a reality of loss: young people die.

On the surface, this is an anecdote. But remembering this story reignited my anger at how the clerk's narrow perspective inflicted pain. This angry moment generated a written scene about the fundamental agony of those post-tragedy phone calls, and the hurt that comes in having to tell your truth over and over.

Write what you remember. Start there. Then write about what you want to remember, but don't. We'll cover ways to write about what you don't remember later in the book, but you can start at any time you like.

> TIP: That brain-spark phase we discussed in the last section
> is an ongoing part of writing, even after you've determined
> your memoir's plot. You'll be writing along swimmingly, and
> a scene will trigger an idea, and you'll find that you have to
> divert and go back to the journal or that you'll want to open
> a new file on your hard drive and explore what this new idea
> means to you. Maybe what you write will fit neatly into the
> beginning, middle, or end that you've already found, or maybe
> it will send you in a new direction. Welcome that new idea,
> even if it acts like the bratty kid who won't play well with the
> others you've written. They might learn to get along.

When my memoir manuscript lacked background information about why my father and I had become estranged, I needed
other eyes to see that my plot and characters relied on that part
of the story. It's one thing to say we barely talked for years, but
it's better writing to show what happened.

Over lunch with my agent and my editor, I related what I
considered just a typical-for-him anecdote about Dad's excus-
ing himself from Sarah's shiva—the after-burial Jewish ritual
when family members receive guests at home. After a short
time, he got ready to leave, telling my mother and me that the
day would be too painful for him. As guests watched him go to
the door, my years of anger at my father overwhelmed me, and
I confronted him.

Over lunch, the attentive faces of my editor and agent
showed me that I'd uncovered the beginnings of a scene. There
was writing to be done, but the idea had emerged from some
hidden, pissed-off place where it lay, until telling it to myself and
others led me to see how it fit in my story. Here's an excerpt of
how that anger took shape in the memoir.

> I called out to my father over the steady hum of conversa-
> tions and the insistent ringing phone. "Are you leaving?"
> I asked.

I was angry. Sarah had been dead less than two days. Her family and friends were inert with grief, and our father seemed to have other things to do.

He held up his hands, a gesture of surrender, and walked toward me. His actions pleaded, "Lower your voice. Let's not make a scene."

These are my memories of my mother's living room that afternoon. The presence of ambient sound in this passage represented by the conversation and ringing phone, as well as words like "hum" and "insistent," infuse the characters' rising anger into the scene's tense environment and dialogue. In addition to the sounds, the image of my father walking toward me with his hands in the air invites the reader in to the emotional distance and inversion of power in that moment between the characters of my father and me.

The Right Voice

Your voice is one of the most important tools you bring to writing your memoir. Voice lets a reader know in the first few paragraphs who she has agreed to settle in with for the next few hundred pages: if you're strident, angry, whiny, serious, formal, funny, or relaxed. A voice on paper isn't audible, but your word choice and pacing bring your personality immediately to the page and into the reader's mind.

In writing memoir, particularly about something as painful as grief and loss, voice isn't pretense. Voice is one of the first agreements you make with yourself about how you will manage your writing craft. The voice you have now is shaped in some way by your loss, which can sometimes be hard for you to reckon with. It may be wiser, or funnier, or more perceptive than you expect. But letting that voice out onto the page is part of identifying yourself in the days and years after your loss.

Your writer's voice comes about as part of acknowledging that the original trauma itself is in the past.

Developing voice is a matter of practice. Your writing voice will differ depending on the piece you're writing, on the topic, and the readership you want to reach. If you are accustomed to writing in an academic or technical style, a grief memoir will naturally need different word choices and phrasing structures because of the different emotional connections for you. If you traditionally write holiday round-up letters informing far-flung relatives of the year's news, that voice is probably a chatty, breezy one, not the thoughtful or passionate voice you reveal to yourself in your journals. Your voice will change again if you write humor, journalism, fiction, or children's stories.

Memoirist and naturalist Janisse Ray writes in her memoir, *Drifting into Darien: A Personal and Natural History of the Altamaha River* about attending a meeting at which a representative from an energy policy group makes a statement with which she vehemently disagrees.

> The speaker actually boasted that burning down our forests will reduce greenhouse gases as well as air pollution. You name me a wood fire that doesn't give off CO_2 and I'll eat a church pew.

In this scene, Ray is appalled. You know this from the adverb "actually," which almost lets you hear her exasperation as clearly as if you were at that meeting with her. Her language is direct, unadorned, factual, and idiomatic. Even if we've never heard her speak, we know this is her real voice. Her relationship to the natural environment is crucial to all of her writing, and by speaking plainly in this scene, she invites the reader to care as strongly as she does. Ray is from Georgia, and in this excerpt she uses a sentence structure that's often heard in Southern speech: "You name me a wood fire . . ."—and describes impossibility in a way that's infuriated and humorous at the same time—". . . I'll eat a church pew." One of the reasons I like this passage so much is the apparent lack of artifice in her voice. Ray doesn't write in a way that feels forced. Her impassioned, conversational tone brings me immediately into her story, and if I didn't already feel as she does in this scene, I would easily be convinced.

"A reader doesn't experience emotion just because you do," Ray explained when we talked about this passage. "The reader experiences emotion because you've translated that feeling into art." In this instance of voice, she notes that it's deliberately clear that she's angry, and she's applied her authority and life experience to bringing her feelings to the page.

Whether or not you have already written one book, several, or none at all, you have the necessary authority about your own life experience to put words on the page, and to use the craft of voice to create art.

Sue William Silverman, in her memoir *Because I Remember Terror, Father, I Remember You*, writes about being sexually abused by her father from the time she was four until she was eighteen. In this excerpt, her voice is an innocent one, using her perspective as a small child, but the increasing length and complexity of the sentences builds a sense of menace and contrast between the fantasy world upstairs, where she is, and the implication of violence downstairs, where her father is.

I am four and pretend I am an Egyptian princess. For this game I arrange planks of wood across my parents' brown-and-white checked bedspread. The wood becomes a tributary of the Nile River, and as I flee across the bank, escaping, someone is chasing me. Downstairs in the living room, my father builds furniture with his electric saw, a gleaming metal table with a round, jagged blade, whirring as it nears the wood, whirring as it severs a plank gripped in a vise. I believe I hear the wood screaming, the metal slicing faster.

For Silverman, a memoirist has two voices: the "Voice of Innocence" and the "Voice of Experience," names she adopted from early nineteenth-century poet and engraver William Blake's *Songs of Innocence and of Experience*. Silverman explained to me that the voice of innocence relates the facts of the story, "who you were and what you felt at the time the events occurred." But in well-written grief memoirs, raw emotion isn't the whole story. Musing on what happened and how it's changed you is the story. The voice of experience, in Silverman's terminology, examines what the innocent self remembers and puts it in context through metaphor, research, and experience.

So every night I must believe, truly believe, my body is swaddled in soft ginger and hibiscus petals, slowly curling inward for night, protecting me from dark spirits of night.

In this example from Silverman's memoir, her innocent voice describes the hibiscus flower. Later in the book, in the experienced voice, Silverman recognizes that as a victimized child, she emotionally removed herself from her father's abuse by imagining herself folding up like the flower does in the dark.

For me, a grief memoirist's two voices work together like harmony and melody. Melody is the tune, and harmony is the musical notes that support and expand on that tune. Imagine the sound of Lennon and McCartney, Emmylou Harris and anyone else, a symphony chorale singing Handel's *Messiah*, or a Gospel choir. These two or more voices create tension and release as the music flows. They are motion themselves.

TIP: To find your voice as you write about what has caused you grief and anger, listen actively to the way you speak about your story when you're comfortable. Then notice when your writing feels most natural to you. Are those two voices, the literal and the figurative, similar in any way? Turn to the authors you truly enjoy reading and ask yourself why their writing appeals to you. When reading this way, you can get under the hood, so to speak, and study how these authors achieved their voice and style. Some of that is the way their particular personalities come through in their word choices, the length and flow of their sentences and paragraphs, and what they choose to focus on and what they prefer to summarize. If the particulars of their story were yours, how would you write the story in your own voice? For example Nancy Mairs, in memoirs and essays like *Plaintext: Deciphering a Woman's Life* writes with a voice that's fierce and direct. Michelle Tea's voice crackles with immediacy in her memoir *The Chelsea Whistle.* In *Lucky,* writing of her rape at age eighteen and the pursuit of justice in the legal system, Alice Sebold's voice is sober and precise.

Some writers prefer not to read other books in their genre when they are deep in the process of writing or are merely contemplating their next work. Some choose not to read other books at all. They worry that another author's voice or technique will distract them or cloud their thinking and creativity. You may find that reading a selection of other memoirs is calming, reassuring, and inspiring. In writing grief memoir, it's helpful to be reminded by the presence of other books that the hard work can be done. That's the calming part. You may be reassured when you read a memoir and realize that if it were your book, you might write this part or that part differently. Maybe you feel you could write it a little better, or maybe it's already so good that you're invigorated by that writer's dazzling skill. And that's where the inspiration comes in. Your voice is different than another writer's because you are a different person. Your experiences, interests, word choices, and phrasing contribute to how you write. They're singular to your story.

Imagine this scenario: It's the first day of school in an elementary classroom, and the teacher makes that venerable "what I did on my summer vacation" assignment. For some reason, all the kids had the same summer vacation, and so they all set out to write in their big lined tablets about the same experience. But when they hand them in, every paper will be different, because every kid has a different voice.

What's Your Point of View?

Most traditional memoirs are written in the first-person point of view, with the author using "I" and "me" to tell their stories. This is the standard in commercial memoir. If your goal is to see your work published, agents and publishers are likely to prefer a memoir written this way. However, some established writers have on occasion delved into second person or third person for sections of their memoir. For example, Abigail Thomas writes in third person in this single-paragraph chapter, "Nothing Under Her Hood" (one of many short chapters in the book) from her memoir *Safekeeping: Some True Stories from a Life.*

> She wasn't like a car. You couldn't open her hood and tinker around. Besides, there wouldn't have been anything under her hood. Just empty space. She was afraid that there was no herself, that somehow she had gotten into this body, but that she was too small for it, tiny. She was fooling people who thought she was real, and here. Her husband used to say, "But we are all nothing. None of us is anything at all." But she didn't know what he meant by that.

Thomas used the third-person voice because, she explained to me, "there are some things you can't write about in the first person without sounding like a victim, or whiny, or an angel." She says that she wasn't conscious of choosing which pieces in the book needed to be in a particular voice, but she did try the passages in different ways before she settled on a point of view. "There were things I tried in the first person that sounded to my ears like bragging or like feeling sorry for myself," she explained, which led her to try an alternate voice. She compares third person to a different way of seeing. "Third person can give you the distance you need, almost as if by looking through the wrong end of a telescope you can see yourself more clearly."

Some of the pieces were unbearably hard to write in anything but the third person, she added, emphasizing that a writer can try to make a moment have a more universal feeling by using third person instead of first.

As a rule, though—and rules can be broken, as Thomas's example demonstrates—third person is rarely used in memoir, unless, of course, the author is referring to another person. That shift in pronoun from "I" to "she" is likely to imply that you've given away the authority to tell your own story. If you're a risk-taker, third person or even second person—calling yourself "you"—can be an interesting technique to try out as short passages as you write drafts of your memoir, or work on your journals, brain-sparks, and drafts. Second person is a deliberate way to show on the page that you're creating distance from the character of yourself, as in a dream sequence or a real-life incident of trauma when you do feel dissociated from your body. But this technique can also work against you, leaving the reader feeling disconnected from your character and unable to empathize with your story.

First Person: How the "I" Sees

Writing in first person is the gold standard in memoir. "The 'I' is a persona that guides the reader," says Michael Steinberg, author of the memoir *Still Pitching*, writing professor, and founding editor of the award-winning literary journal *Fourth Genre: Explorations in Nonfiction*. In this excerpt from his memoir, *Still Pitching*, the reader meets Steinberg's adult "I" persona as he looks back on the boy he was.

For as long as I could remember, my mother, an ex-preschool teacher, was a voracious reader. I recall that a lot of books, newspapers, and magazines—like *Reader's Digest* condensed editions, dictionaries and encyclopedias, *Sunday Times, Life, Colliers, Harper's, New Yorker,* and *Saturday Evening Post*—were always strewn around all over our kitchen table and living room floor.

According to her I was an avid reader and bright, curious kid. Maybe that's how I seemed at home. But in school I was shy, scared, and withdrawn.

The author's "I" persona here—his voice—is a tender, ruminative one. He looks back across time and names the popular reading material in his childhood home, not only on the table but on the floor. And then he contrasts, without high drama, the difference between the way his mother said she remembered him ("according to her") in those days, and what he knew about himself that was different. The roots of conflict are present. A story begins.

First-person voice is sometimes used in fiction, but in memoir, the first-person point of view—the "I"—announces to the reader that the book in his hands is a true story told by the author. Using the "I" pronoun is conversational, confessional, intimate, and claims irrefutably that you are the authority on what happened in your life. Because if you aren't, who is?

Leading a trauma-writing workshop for a dozen women in the living room of a comfortable farmhouse retreat, I asked each writer in the group to take a few moments and write a scene in which she was traveling from one location to another. The task was to include sensory details, write in first person, and let us know what we're seeing through your eyes as narrator and protagonist.

When the writing time was up, we went around the room and each woman read her draft. One woman had written in third person out of habit. In her draft, "she" experienced her travel, described what "she" saw, and how it made "her" feel.

"Try it in first person," I suggested. Change the "she" and "her" to "I" and "me."

The writer hesitated. "I couldn't," she said. "It's just too scary." A few of the women in the workshop agreed. Identifying yourself on the page as yourself—as "I" or "me"—can seem awkward and even frightening to a writer new to memoir. Starting too many sentences with "I" or "me" might feel as if you're bragging, dominating a conversation, or calling attention to yourself. If the emotions or interactions you're writing about are negative in some way, claiming them with that personal pronoun can be even more uncomfortable. But that doesn't necessarily make using the "I" pronoun the wrong thing to do. Taking possession of that pronoun might be your first step toward writing frankly about your grief. As you develop scene and character in your memoir, you'll recognize ways to balance how you use the "I" pronoun on the page. Of course every sentence shouldn't start that way. As you continue to place your story in the wider world, a subtle balance will appear in your writing. Go ahead and write "I"—this is your story.

Other women in the workshop that day had accepted the challenge eagerly, and found that they were comfortable referring to themselves on the page as they would in speech, using "I" and "me." As a group, we encouraged the writer who had found first person difficult to try again on her own, and keep trying until she felt comfortable writing about herself as "I." She was intrigued, and agreed to keep trying.

Writing a story in first person point of view—the "I" voice—is traditional in memoir, but it does have limitations that a writer has to look out for. For example, writing about real life this way means that you can't get inside another character's head and know what's on their mind. You can't know how that person views the world unless they demonstrate that information through speech or action. You're obliged to set the scene for the reader and place yourself within a larger context. But how do you do that if "I" can only know what's in "my" mind?

Stories of grief, loss, and trauma are by nature self centered, but infusing your story with the vitality and strength to connect with others means writing a scene so that it takes place as it actually did, in the wider world. As a writer, of course you want to enliven the interactions between characters on the page. One way to do that is write past simply identifying the other people in your scene by name or writing their dialogue. For example, a description like "Peter looked at me," or a line of dialogue like "I got a postcard!" doesn't have the same impactful sense of place and emotion as, "Peter was out of breath when he grabbed my hand and told me that he'd gotten a postcard from Bill." While these examples remain in the first person, the added description lets the reader experience the scene with the same emotions as the protagonist, from the protagonist's point of view.

This way, as a writer recapturing a traumatic event, you've moved beyond summary into scene, and put your reader into that difficult moment with you so that they can really see, hear, and start to understand what happened. We read your writing and know that Peter is breathless, he holds the protagonist's hand, and that the postcard matters, if not to both of them, then certainly to Peter.

As you write in first person, include names, relationships, and scenic description so that you bring the story out of your inner world and place the characters in a sensory, physical environment.

But in the example of Peter and the postcard, we're still not inside Peter's head. In order to convey what he's thinking, you would have had to interview the real Peter about what was on his mind at that moment, or have read his letters or diaries with an eye toward reconstructing his personal insights about that particular postcard. What if you can't or don't chose to do that? That's when you bring in other aspects of your experience in order to write nonfiction about what you don't know.

What If You Don't Know Why

As you write about grief or trauma, it can seem particularly important that you know why something happened or what was on someone else's mind when their actions affected you. That "why" and "how" are part of your story, but you don't always have the answers. You can speculate, but in order to maintain the authority inherent in that personal pronoun "I," guessing must be identified as what it is—guessing. Signal phrases like "I imagine" or "I believe" free you to speculate as an author. They also let the reader know that's what you're doing. Signal phrases are memoir craft in action. Here's an example of a signal phrase from Darin Strauss's memoir, *Half a Life*.

> I don't remember how long we'd all been there, whether
> I'd gone to look at Celine's excessively pale face again.

In this scene, he is a teenager, and has stepped out of the car he was driving. He has just accidently hit a bicyclist, a girl from his school. Writing "I don't remember" at the beginning of the sentence frees Strauss from having to write something he surely doesn't know and can't find out—the accurate number of seconds or minutes that passed between his exiting the car and approaching the injured girl. The signal phrase does something else, too. It conveys for the reader the free-floating, suspended feeling that often accompanies great fear.

That "I" pronoun represents two aspects of you: the you who's writing now, and the you who experienced grief sometime in the past. When I talked with Michael Steinberg about his approach to memoir in writing *Still Pitching*, he commented that "the experience of the writer at the desk is that "I" looking back on the earlier version of him or herself, trying to understand that earlier version of the character of 'me.'"

When Memories Differ

What happens when you remember something differently than another person? Which one of you is right? What if you're both right? What's emotionally true for you may not have the ring of truth for others who were present in the same situation. Whether someone else's version of events angers you or gives you insight, claiming your perspective on events that matter to you is another place where the confidence to tell your story of loss comes in. Remember that writing simply to make a point in anger or to seek revenge diminishes your writing. It's your story, but examining other perspectives brings balance to your memoir, and more completely re-creates the real world in which your story took place.

MY STORY:

My paternal grandmother was kind to me. She was prickly and opinionated, but I don't dispute her love. My sister Sarah disagreed with me, and she liked that grandmother less. The reason is simple: That grandmother seemed to be harder on Sarah than she was on me. Her reasons are lost to me; she died when I was in college and Sarah was in junior high school. What caused her differing opinions about her grandchildren I can never know.

But the verifiable facts are the same. Her name was Rosalie. She had scoliosis as a child in the early years of the twentieth century, and ever after had a curved spine. She used Jean Naté bath splash, and its spicy scent surrounded her all day. She and our grandfather had two children: our father and our aunt. I could still point out to you the two-story white Colonial-revival house in Harrisburg, Pennsylvania, that had been their home, and if

Susie and Sarah were alive, they could, too. We could all go feed the ducks on the small public lake that abutted the backyard. But our perceptions of our relationship with her? Purely personal, derived from our own emotions and memories. Sarah and I would each be right about our different impressions of and relationship with our grandmother. And if our grandmother were alive, she would offer a third perspective.

Dialogue: What Did He Say?

Readers don't expect a memoirist to present verbatim every conversation she ever had. It's a common understanding that in memoir, an author reconstructs dialogue using the best of her ability. Word-for-word precision just isn't possible, especially as the conversations themselves fade into the past. You may be frustrated by not remembering someone's exact words, but try to view that absence of information as an opportunity to learn more about how to depict a character beyond his or her precise spoken words. You'll notice a disclaimer at the front of many of your favorite memoirs that says something along the lines of "dialogue is presented as I remembered it." That is also the place in the book where, if the author has changed the names of some of her characters, she points that out in a statement like "some names and identifying details have been changed." Consider these disclaimers as evidence that memoir as a genre accepts that memory is fallible and subjective.

What a reader does expect is that the author make his best effort to capture the meaning of the conversation, as well as the tone and some of the important traits of the way the character spoke. Conversations in real life are full of repetition, pauses, and digressions. Our conversations are usually going somewhere, but very often, they take the long route. People in face to face conversation or on the phone often don't finish sentences. They say "er" and "um" while they think or stall for time. A person talking *around* grief, rather than talking *about* it, might try to change the subject to spare themselves having to deliver bad news or having to hear it. When we cry or lament, we repeat ourselves, often insensibly.

Will these natural ways of speaking hold up on the page? Generally not in their entirety. A little bit of dialogue that represents stalling or talking around something goes a long way for a reader, and makes your point quickly. The noises that a speaker uses to fill a pause, like "er" or "um," don't work at all on the page. That's where scenic, visual writing comes in. When a person stalls while they're delivering information that will bring grief, try to notice or remember what they do to busy themselves physically. They might avoid eye contact, or suddenly become preoccupied with rummaging through their handbag, or reading street signs aloud if they're in a moving car.

Because talking about loss and grief is uncomfortable for many people, and in my family, was almost never done, these passages of dialogue might naturally be few and far between. Sparse dialogue has a great deal of value in a grief memoir. These spoken words that come with exceptional emotion are rare jewels when we reconstruct them for the page. You might find those snippets of dialogue hard to remember or impossible to forget. You may not remember a crucial conversation at all.

For writers of grief memoir, there are specific conversations or fragments of discussions that never leave us: the boss's words when she closes your division and leaves you without a job, the neighbor's call identifying a dead dog as your lost Prince. This is direct dialogue—those phrases between quotation marks. When you use direct dialogue on the page, you bring the reader closely into an exchange between characters. Well-chosen dialogue can make the fire of your story flare up and the emotional heat intensify: the reader is right there, a fly on the wall of a conversation in real time, as close to "as it happened" as possible.

Poorly written or overused dialogue can do the opposite, isolating the reader from the action by being *too* talky.

Writing conversations as dialogue can make a scene active and vital. Here's an example from the very beginning of *Invisible Sisters*, as Sarah and I discuss the plans for a bone marrow transplant that, in the absence of a suitable donor, never took place.

> " 'That's not what I'm talking about,' Sarah said. When I die—that's what I mean."
>
> I made comforting noises, demurring. You won't die from this, don't be silly, this will work, this time will save your life.
>
> "When I die," Sarah said, suddenly fierce, "you will be the only one left."

Of course I don't remember every word that my sister and I said to each other throughout our lives, but I do remember the direct dialogue in this conversation so clearly that I can still feel the plastic phone receiver against my cheek and hear Sarah's voice in my ear. Every day that actual conversation recedes further into my past, but I will never forget those exact words and how they made me feel.

As you write dialogue, pay attention to the physical and emotional details that accompany the spoken word. Don't be afraid or ashamed if you write very little dialogue in emotional scenes. Sometimes silence says more than words. Write that someone was silent if that's how you remember them. Write what they didn't say, what you wanted them to say (remember to use signal phrases), or how they physically delivered or withheld information.

Conversely, if your memoir—or a portion of it—is full of talk, try to evaluate where and when dialogue can do the most effective work for your story. A naturally talkative character is represented throughout the memoir by the quantity—and quality—of what they say. A reticent person really makes a mark when they do speak up.

Just as in a film, characters don't stand still and flap their lips. There is a wealth of information for the author and the reader in a person's physical behavior when they speak, if they're using slang or formal speech, and the emotional charge in their words and actions.

For example, in his memoir *The Boy in the Moon,* Ian Brown writes of watching his wife, who has, for an evening, emerged from "the cocoon of her endless obligations" involved in caring for their severely developmentally delayed son, Walker. At a social gathering, she converses with an old friend, and Brown describes watching her across a room, drinking vodka tonics with a man they both know. He writes of her smile, her laugh, and of his pleasure in watching his wife and a mutual friend enjoying themselves, which he observes that his wife has lately been unable to do.

Paul Guest, in his memoir *One More Theory About Happiness,* brings the sound of a personal care assistant's voice, as well as the man's diction, enthusiasm, and physicality to the page. Guest, who is quadriplegic, has just started graduate school in a new city, and with his mother is interviewing candidates for the job of personal assistant. The list of names to call is long, and the responses have been disappointing. At the end of a long day, they make another phone call, and a man answers.

He spoke with what I guessed was an Eastern European accent.

"Yes, yes, what is it?" he said loudly. A woman yelled in the background and I was silent while he yelled back. "What do you want? Who is calling me today?"

He spoke quickly, almost too quickly to follow, his words smashing up against one another, but in an oddly formal way, with surplus verbiage scattered throughout. Every sentence rose to a little giggle, as if its true meaning were a secret amusement.

I explained to him what I needed and what I didn't need. He interrupted me.

"I did this," he barked. "Do not fear: I am your man!"

I paused a second, closing my eyes. He would be the one. I was certain, rueful, intrigued. "You've worked with quadriplegics before?"

"Many!" he shouted, excited.

Guest has made the character of Lazar Tonu, whom we later learn prefers to be called "Tony," hurtle from the page in a kinetic tumult. His manic energy comes through in the words Guest chooses to describe Tony's speech—words that behave in ways Guest writes as "smashing" and "scattered"—as well as Tony's interruptions as Paul explains what he will require of him.

Guest told me that in person, Tony was "intensely physical, and that came across in every aspect of him. He could hardly sit still or be quiet, and his speech was an artifact of that physicality." In addition, his job requirements were physical. "He was bathing me, dressing me, there was a connection to the body on both our parts that came out in the language," he explained.

Guest, who is originally from Tennessee, chose not to write Tony's dialogue using an attempt at Tony's Romanian accent. "A person who speaks English as a second language has their own way of expressing themselves," he explains. "In writing, it's easy to not truly convey it in a way that's respectful or accurate." He compares his capturing of Tony's dialogue to a translation. He suggests to the reader his own experience of listening to Tony through small amounts of phrasing and behavior, and lets a reader's mind fill in the blanks.

Guest's use of the word "rueful" as he describes evaluating his potential aide reads at first as a slight discordance in a sentence that otherwise demonstrates conviction. The word hints at the protagonist's—the author's—internal conflict.

At the time *One More Theory About Happiness* was written, Guest had worked with personal aides for more than twenty years. He explained to me, "If you want to hire a plumber you can open the Yellow Pages and get someone to do the job and not destroy the house, but you never know what you're going to get when you turn your body over to someone." While many aides are wonderful, others don't always engage in the best working relationship. "After going through this for years and years," he says, "you have a sense of what to dread, and that's where the ruefulness comes in." In choosing to include his mixed emotions in words like "certain, rueful, intrigued," Guest brings the reader back to the protagonist's—his own—point of view and authority in the story.

How to Swear, Use Foreign Languages, and Other Conundrums

Here again you'll want to consider the details of how a person spoke. The person whose speech you're trying to re-create may have spoken with a thick accent, been new to English, peppered their speech with catchphrases, or have been someone who, like me, swears all the time. Perhaps they're someone who swears so rarely that when they do curse, people around them quake in fear.

For example, my father often used Yiddish, the language of his grandparents, for expletives. Like many people of his generation, whose parents or grandparents emigrated from Eastern Europe in the last years of the nineteenth century and the first decade of the twentieth century, he hardly knew the language. The generation before his tended to use their Yiddish, which they had learned as children, to discuss subjects they didn't want to share with their own children. What their children picked up, more often than not, were short phrases of invectives, exclamations, and endearments rather than full and complex sentences. When I think of my father's angry outbursts, I still hear the harsh tones of a curse word, his American sounding, mid-Atlantic accented Yiddish, and later, the smooth baritone of his voice when it calmed.

Writing the characteristics of someone's way of speaking gives you and the reader insight into that person and the emotion in the scene. Capturing accents, vernacular speech, the lilt or rasp in a tone, even malapropisms like "frolicles" for "follicles" lets you bring these characters to life on the page through the personality of their speech.

Most readers recognize common phrases from other languages if they're written in the Roman alphabet. Memoirs of loss and grief often involve family going back generations, which means, in the United States, that memoirs may include the stories of family members who emigrated from or remained in non-English-speaking countries. A story of war will involve the language of the country in which the war is fought. Professions like medicine, law, and science can bring another kind of language into play: jargon, the terminology used in a profession that can seem foreign to someone unfamiliar with the words.

Just a *soupçon* of unfamiliar words places a reader into the scene and invites her into the setting and the sound of the conversation you're writing. A reader will comprehend a new word's general meaning from the sentence itself. This is called "content from context." The French word I used at the beginning of this paragraph means "a bit." If you're not familiar with French, you still might have heard the word or seen it used in a recipe. Even if you haven't, if you stuck with this paragraph, you probably got the idea. Longer phrases should be translated or paraphrased so that the reader's involvement in your story doesn't waver.

Words written in alphabets that an English-language reader might not recognize pose a different challenge. A language like Thai, Russian, Greek, or Hebrew written as it appears untranslated gives the reader a strong visual sense of difference, otherness, and community. But unless the writer provides a translation immediately afterward, or the reader is familiar with the language and its alphabet, the writer's meaning is lost. For example, if you're writing about a letter, a road sign, or a newspaper written in characters that aren't in the Roman alphabet (the alphabet used in English) you may want to describe what the lettering looked like to you. Perhaps it reassured you that you were home, or if you couldn't read it, maybe the lettering seemed curly as lace or angular as tiles. If the content of the sign or newspaper matters to your story, let the reader know what it said and how the message got through to you despite the unfamiliar writing.

> TIP: Perhaps your conversations are or were in a language other than English, and you speak that language well. Or you spoke a language poorly and struggled to grasp what people around you were saying. Maybe you thought you understood and a mishap, good or bad, ensued. What scenes can you develop from a moment in your story of loss when two languages were spoken?

MY STORY:

I have a family photograph of a teenaged boy from around the time my maternal grandfather came to America (I'm presuming this from the clothing and architecture in the picture). On the back of the photo are four lines of handwriting in faded blue ink. I wish I knew what the message said, but it's in cursive Yiddish. No one I know can read it, including the older people in my family and my husband's family. "It's cursive," they say, dismissively. They spoke some Yiddish as children, but were reading English by the time they graduated to cursive handwriting.

Because I can't read the writing, I can only describe it: looks to me like short vertical arcs and loops, as if it were made from kitten claws and eyelashes. I don't know who the little boy grew up to be, who wrote the note on the back, or where in the world they are. I don't know why they're there.

I can only write about this boy using the first-person pronoun, because I don't know anything about his internal life, and don't know who I can ask. Instead, I can write about what I don't know and the very little that I do. He's wearing a jacket and tie and a brimmed cap. He is standing on a beach. There are several ornate buildings in the background: they're probably bathhouses or a hotel. Another person in the shot reclines on the sand, resting his head in his hand. Our boy is smiling. His hands are in his trouser pockets, his tie is askew. Because this image dates from the time of my grandfather's emigration from Russia, I imagine this image is of my grandfather or a great-uncle, and that the handwriting is his mother's or even grandmother's. From here, he looks too young for a girlfriend. Even though I can't read the language that accompanies the image, I can write about my reactions to the image, and why those reactions lead me to believe the photo is a part of my larger story.

Scratch the Surface of the Story and Find . . . Another Story

In Robin Hemley's memoir, *Do-Over!* he chronicles his return, as a forty-eight-year-old father of three, to ten events in his life that caused him regret the first time around. One aspect of the book, he said in an interview with *Failure Magazine,* was to encourage readers to consider how their failures shaped them, and to try to reconnect with people they had left behind. In *Do-Over!* he suggests that sometimes a writer of memoir has to reconsider certain things he's tried to leave behind, in order to see who he's become as he's grown, especially if some of those events "linger in our minds as disasters."

On his quest, Hemley attended kindergarten again (briefly), attended prom at his former high school (with a date), reprised his role in a school play, and participated in what he calls reenactments of seven other life events that had troubled him. Writing in *A Field Guide for Immersion Writing: Memoir, Journalism, and Travel*, he explains why he tackled *Do-Over!*

> What was at stake?
>
> In other words, what was my motivation for writing the book? It couldn't be because . . . I like to see my name on a book jacket. In any memoir . . . there has to be something more substantial at stake emotionally for the writer.

Later he writes:

> You should always ask yourself "what's the story here?" and then "What's the real story?" Conceptualizing in such a way adds texture to your story, layers it, makes it seem more than simply a superficial treatment of your subject.

Hemley's question about the story and the real story is another way to talk about the nominal story and the substantive story, or what's happening and what it's really about. "If you're writing memoir," Hemley told me, "you've built up many defenses over the years, against your own fears and secrets and things you are embarrassed or nervous about other people finding out." He encourages memoir writers to engage in detective work about their own lives. He told me that "the first detective act is to try to peer through the keyhole into who you really are. Figure out why you're telling the story in the first place, and who is this person telling the story."

Where Do You Begin?

Where you begin your memoir of loss matters to you and to your reader. The first pages of your memoir are also the first moments the reader spends with you and your story. The scene you choose to place first sets the tone, establishes your voice, and focuses your story, implicitly telling the reader who and what the memoir is about on the deepest level. A beginning can also hint at how the memoir will end. Consider the bravery with which Darin Strauss begins his memoir *Half a Life*: a statement that allows no going back once it's been read.

> Half my life ago, I killed a girl.

With this frank sentence, Strauss cuts his life into two parts, and on the very first page tells the reader what the book will be about. It will be about him, and it will be about another person, the girl. We will have to read further to learn her name, what happened, how, and why. We don't know yet why he has waited half his life to tell the story. The sentence itself is in two pieces evenly split on either side of a comma. Even if we don't stop to examine the physical characteristics of the sentence, we can sense that balance and imbalance will be the deeper story in this memoir of loss. At the ending of the memoir, that promise of exploring balance is adjusted again, as he writes, using the phrase "half a life" again, that the tragedy is not only his, but also belongs to the girl who was killed. In doing so, he echoes that first sentence of his memoir and establishes the sense of a full circle.

Lee Martin's memoir about his childhood, *From Our House*, begins with what appears to be an anecdote about his father's shortening his own name, a story that the reader doesn't immediately realize introduces the idea of truncation, of shortening or doing without. Here are the first sentences of the book.

My father, when he was a boy, took it upon himself to change his name. My grandparents had named him Leroy Martin, but when he went to school and started learning cursive handwriting, he had trouble forming a capital "L." His answer to the problem was to drop the first two letters of his name and become, from then on, "Roy." . . . So began his method for confronting obstacles with swift and decisive action.

As you read on, however, the memoir's true intentions become clear. The loss on which the memoir pivots is the amputation of Roy Martin's two hands, and his son's—the author's—reckoning with understanding a father changed in an instant by trauma.

"I started with a fact," Martin explained to me. "It's what he did with his name, but as soon as I wrote that on the page, I had a sense somewhere inside me that it was representative of his whole life, and specifically of the loss that he would suffer and would radiate throughout the whole family."

In the last chapter of the memoir, Martin's father does something unusual for him. He accompanies his wife and son to church. Martin writes about his father's baptism, and in doing so, writes of his father's overcoming another obstacle in his life. In this passage, Martin subtly reminds the reader of the physical imagery that drives his father's anger: his amputated hands.

When he was baptized, he went down into the water without his hooks, the weathered flesh of one stump on Luther Tolliver's hand that held a folded handkerchief to my father's nose.

That "sense" Martin speaks about isn't magic. He began the memoir as a series of essays. The essay that became the opening chapter originally started differently, with what is now the second paragraph of the first page, a straightforward telling of the farming accident itself.

Another memoir, *The Memory of All That: George Gershwin, Kay Swift, and My Family's Legacy of Infidelities* touches on many generations in a wide-reaching family tree, but author Katharine Weber wanted to begin and end in her own experience, the lens through which she will see the history of her family. She begins with a beach scene from the early 1960s, that depicts herself, her father, and her mother.

> We are walking into the ocean. He is holding me in the crook of his left arm and I cling awkwardly to the soft expanse of his chest where I am squashed against his cold skin and his disconcerting chest hair. He wades deeper into the black water that laps against my thighs, and I am afraid, afraid of him and afraid of the ocean. He strides through the waves, a father going into the ocean with his little girl, and over his shoulder I see my mother in her blue seersucker shorts and her dark blue sleeveless shirt standing on the wet sand at the hem of the tide, taking photographs, her face masked by her perpetual Leica as she frames her picture of a devoted father holding his happy child.

"The beach was a profound early memory of my father, [and of] depending on someone undependable. I remember being trapped with him in an endless process of trying to escape. I wanted these pages to function as an invitation to the reader to come wade into the water with me," Weber explains. She adds that the passage subtly presents the idea that "he's untrustworthy, but you can trust me." She makes this idea clear through words like "squashed," "cold," and "disconcerting," as well as the growing distance between the girl and her mother as the father wades farther out. The reader's sense of unease complicates as Weber describes the image of her mother photographing them for "her picture [the mother's perception] of a devoted father holding his happy child."

In another example of starting with a small detail that

gains deeper meaning as the reader progresses, Abigail Thomas's memoir *A Three Dog Life* begins with a sense of solidity within turmoil, but for her, it's the trauma that's stable, and daily life that shifts.

> This is the one thing that stays the same: my husband got hurt. Everything else changes. A grandson needs me and then he doesn't. My children are close then one drifts away. I smoke and don't smoke; I knit ponchos, then hats, shawls, hats again, stop knitting, start up again.

This section was initially the last piece Thomas wrote for the book, but she says that it "just felt right" as the opening. She liked the tone set by the interaction between "the serious playing with the funny."

Kathryn Rhett begins *Near Breathing: A Memoir of a Difficult Birth*, with a prologue that takes place later in her life when her daughter is a toddler. Rhett and her daughter take in the view of Cape Cod Bay from a hilltop cemetery in their town, and Rhett muses on the page that:

> There are gravestones for children everywhere, many of the nineteenth century inscriptions still legible. Of the worn inscriptions, I can make out a Millie, a Lizzie, and two who died in the years of their births, 1845 and 1855. The sun is hot today, wilting the dandelions, sparking crystals in the stones.

At the end of the prologue, she holds her daughter, who has been picking summer vegetables.

> I hold her tightly, feeling lucky. She is three. I expect so much.

The specter of death is present in the gravestones, made personal by names, before it's brought into the present by the vibrancy of the sun and its strength making flowers wilt and crystals sparkle. This is conflict, too: the tacit darkness of death and gravestones against the brilliance and heat of the sun. We see very quickly that her own child is alive, in her arms, and that Rhett, the mother, feels lucky. These conflicts intrigue you as the reader, and encourage you to turn the page and read more.

Rhett started the memoir's narrative at a point after the crisis had resolved because she didn't want readers to wonder if the baby girl had died. "I wanted to place myself in context and say I feel so lucky," she says. "So many babies have died, many women die in childbirth." Beginning the book this way, she explains, is not a bid for sympathy, but an attempt to articulate a life-changing experience.

Middle

I love real, paper maps, although Sarah and I argued about them. My sister found them tedious, but to me, a map is a bird's-eye view of a story. A few years ago I rescued a 1921 atlas from a junk heap. The book's fabric cover, faded to the pink of a cat's tongue and nearly as rough to the touch, poked up from a pile of books and miscellaneous household objects beside a trash can. The atlas is tabloid-sized, with two hundred and seventy-two pages of full-page, fold-out maps of countries, states, and cities. The cover needed a good dose of disinfectant, but the book offered a pleasure I couldn't ignore. Maps tell me stories that I want to read.

The paper map is a disappearing form of storytelling that I grieve in this era of Global Positioning Systems. Global positioning systems are useful if you need to know instantly what turn to take and how many miles are left before you reach your destination, but the device doesn't tell the whole story. A GPS doesn't show you where you are in the city at large, or how the places you've been (and the person you were then) connect to other, more distant places. Nor does it show the phases of the moon, if a city is close to the ocean or the mountains, or what the crops or industry are. Without an actual paper map you might miss wonderful, evocative place names that thrill the imagination, like Cat Head Creek, Georgia; Gladys, Alberta; or Duckwater, Nevada.

Janisse Ray writes in *Ecology of a Cracker Childhood* of maps as both living things and the embodiment of story.

> Not long ago I dreamed of actually cradling a place, as if something so amorphous and vague as a region, existing mostly in imagination and idea, suddenly took form. I held its shrunken relief in my arms, a baby smelted from a plastic topography map, and when I gazed down into its face, as my father had gazed into mine, I saw the pine flatwoods of my homeland.

You can identify the middle of your memoir by imagining your plot as an unfolding map. Your research, your sections and scenes, and even the structural form you choose for your memoir are destinations along the way. As you brain-spark, write scenes, and discover their unifying images, these form the path that your memoir follows as you write your way across the bridge connecting who you were before and after your grief.

TIP: You may already have your plot's map, and merely need to shake it out and look at it. If you took an annual family car trip, you probably have a collection of imaginary mile markers that are surprisingly automatic, such as here's where we always stopped to get ice cream, there's where my brother always got carsick, or after this exit is the welcome center where kids got free plastic straws shaped like alligators with serrated jaws to stick into a fresh orange—welcome to Florida. The mental map of your memoir's plot works in a similarly instinctive way. You've already taken parts of that trip many times. Ask yourself, what stop came next?

MY STORY:

When I was an adult, after living and working in Boston, Los Angeles, and a few stops in between, I made the decision to move back to Atlanta, where my sisters had been alive and we had been children. I returned because as hard as I had tried, I couldn't separate the sounds of our particular Southern accents, my affinity for the grape-gum scent of kudzu in bloom, and the cloaking summer humidity from my identity. Despite the trouble that had happened to my family at this stop on our map, I needed external definitions like these to help me guide myself to the next phase of my life.

But even after I moved back, I kept getting exasperatingly lost in a city I knew well. In order to navigate my route to work, to a friend's house, or to run errands, I had to drive north from my new house for about ten miles and start out again from the street where I'd grown up.

I started writing about my grief by tackling it mile by mile. I didn't look at the total experience of my sisters' absence and the passage of time, but at the white flowers with the burgundy strands on the Bradford pear trees planted in neat rows in front of our childhood home. I thought about how awkward, yet necessary, the task of sitting in my car across the street from what had once been my family's house felt. That's an example of one single mile, not a whole trip.

As a preteen, I'd kept myself from being too homesick at summer camp or on vacations at my grandparents' house in Florida or Pennsylvania by drawing maps of my neighborhood. The maps weren't technically good at all: there were squiggly lines for roads and blobs for yards, squares for houses and bigger squares for schools and stores. I drew stars on the places my friends and I frequented and lines showing our shortcuts through various yards. These maps wouldn't have been useful to anyone actually trying to find their way, but they were tangible confirmation to me that what I knew even then as part of my life story existed: my neighborhood, my friends, or the best spot to stand in the mini-mart to steal wine coolers without being caught.

Drawing a map can be a physical representation of your story's plot. Even a poor map puts your hands on the story. You can move the elements of the plot from your imagination onto a piece of paper so that you can see what's on the path from here to there. On a map, you can assess what obstacles are in your way (that part that you think will be too hard to write), what to work around (the friend who doesn't want you to use her real name), or to make sure that you put in important details where they belong (losing your wedding ring down the shower drain the morning you broke up with your spouse). A map helps you evaluate detours, decide if a digression is valuable to the story, and trace how that roundabout route will bring you back to the main road.

If you've ever been in a car with someone who won't ask directions no matter how many times they cross the same intersection, you know how frustrating not knowing where you're going can be. The same feeling applies to being able to follow even the most general map of your memoir. You and your eventual reader will feel better with a simple reassurance that you're heading in the right direction.

Because I grew up in and live now in the South, I've never grown confident driving in heavy Northern winters. But one winter night, I was driving on Route 7 in rural Western Massachusetts. The snow was falling thick and hard, reflecting my headlights back to me. I couldn't see the road, only whirling snow. I knew the route from Stockbridge to my father's house in a town fewer than ten miles east, but the wall of dizzying white flakes just past the hood of my car made the few miles ahead seem like mist. I might as well have been falling through space.

But I could see a foot or so at a time of yellow dividing line from my side window, and from the steering wheel, I clung to that that yellow line. It was all I could see. Never varying from that line on the road delivered me, jittery and exhilarated, to the place I had set out for.

Find the yellow line in your road that guides you through the story you want to tell. Include whatever turns are necessary, and follow it, mile by mile, to your destination.

And Then What Happened?

The complications come in the middle of a story. These are the twists and turns on the map, or the place where you discover the highway was never finished and you'll have to take a side road. The road is bumpy, or flooded, or wide as a prairie. The story expands. Abigail Thomas's husband suffers a traumatic brain injury and she rebuilds for herself the parameters of their marriage. Marianne Leone's son does well in school despite his disabilities, and then the school system fails him. Kathryn Rhett's first child is endangered at birth, and Kathryn and her husband fear for her future. Nick Flynn meets his lost father in a homeless shelter, and has to decide how to connect with the troubled man.

The same way that a spellbound child on the playground asks the storyteller, "and then what happened?" your reader asks you the same thing. And you, seeking to find your way through grief or understand how you arrived on the other shore, ask yourself that same question. The map you make traces that path.

And then what happened, you ask yourself. What you write

when you answer that question becomes the middle of the story. The map of your plot traces the journey from beginning, through the middle, to the end.

Your loss is the reason you've taken pen to paper. But for your loss to have rewarding meaning to you and to a reader, you're obliged to travel to the substantive depths of your story. As you write your middle, investigate additional story elements that contrast your loss, extend the loss to other characters, or question how and why grief continues to flicker in your life.

In my case, I had my sisters' lives and deaths to write about, and how their illnesses led to my estrangement from our father. I had my childhood and young adulthood to write about. The middle of my memoir was, on the nominal level, about their illnesses and my leaving home. On the substantive level, it was about my fighting and gradually accepting my desire to return. I wrote about going to college, my disastrous romances, moving to Los Angeles, and working behind the scenes in the entertainment industry. And I wrote how I learned to recognize that these were stops on my own journey through grief.

Making a Scene

Marianne Leone, whose memoir *Knowing Jesse: A Mother's Story of Grief, Grace, and Everyday Bliss* tells the story of her son's life with cerebral palsy and his death at seventeen, is also an actor (*The Sopranos, The Three Stooges, City of Hope*.) She explained to me that she was comfortable writing screenplays long before she wrote her memoir. She sees a comparison between writing scenes for the big screen and for prose's theater of the mind.

"You've got to find a way to show character through action and dialogue," she told me. Screenwriting is a visual medium, and because readers conjure images in their heads as they read, so is prose. A reader should easily be able to imagine what you're showing on the page.

Here, she and her son Jesse swim at home on a winter Sunday.

> Jesse is fifteen, waiting patiently in his wheelchair. I lift him out of it, grunting with effort, and lay him down on the table beside the pool. He doesn't weigh much, maybe seventy pounds, but he is all gangly arms and legs that stick out stiffly, sometimes catching on my own arms or legs. I retrieve Jesse's neck float, move him to a sitting position, and awkwardly fit on the float with one hand, supporting his back with the other. I smile at him. He smiles back, anticipating the delight to come. I lift him under his arms and heave him over the side of the pool.
>
> He yelps happily at the sensation of water and weightlessness as the chains of gravity drop away. His tight muscles relax and he kicks his legs. I hold up a CD for approval. "Nelly Furtado?" He clicks "yes." I climb in. We float.

There is no dialogue in the first paragraph, and only two lines of dialogue in the second. But because of the physicality of the action, described through evocative verbs like "lift," "grunting," "retrieve," and "yelps," you as a reader feel as if you're right there by the pool with Marianne and Jesse.

Carefully chosen description makes the scene even more visual. We know what this fifteen-year-old boy weighs, that his limbs "stick out stiffly," that gravity seems to his mother, and we assume to him, like "chains." We know how he communicates—by clicking his tongue—and his taste in music. Writing in unadorned, straightforward language, Leone makes both the physical effort and the pure joy of their afternoon in the pool real to the reader. Notice how that last graceful sentence relaxes a reader much the way it does the characters of Marianne and Jesse in the water.

Many writers consider James Agee's autobiographical novel, *A Death in the Family,* an early example of grief memoir.

The novel, which won the Pulitzer Prize in 1958, tells the story of a young boy, Rufus, (Agee's middle name) and his devotion to his father, whose sudden death in an automobile accident is referenced in the title. Agee died in 1955 before the book was completed. The prologue, written by Agee as a separate essay, was inserted into the book by his editors. That essay, "Knoxville: Summer 1915," first appeared in a magazine called the *Partisan Review* in 1938. In this example from the essay, you can read how it captures scene in a breathtaking way.

> Supper was at six and was over by half past. There was still daylight, shining softly and with a tarnish, like the lining of a shell; and the carbon lamps lifted at the corners were on in the light, and the locusts were started, and the fire flies were out, and a few frogs were flopping in the dewy grass, by the time the fathers and the children came out. The children ran out first hell bent and yelling those names by which they were known; then the fathers sank out leisurely in crossed suspenders, their collars removed and the necks looking tall and shy. The mothers stayed back in the kitchen washing and drying, putting things away, recrossing their traceless footsteps like the lifetime journeys of bees, measuring out the dry cocoa for break-fast. When they came out they had taken off their aprons and their skirts were dampened and they sat in rockers on their porches quietly.

The calm unspooling of detail and the sense of routine, ("recrossing their traceless footsteps like the lifetime journeys of bees") and contentment in this scene and the entire prologue indicates to the reader what will be lost to the boy, giving us the sense of what's about to happen—a transition from calm to life-changing loss.

Robin Hemley, in his first memoir, *Nola: A Memoir of Faith, Art, and Madness,* also sets a scene that foreshadows trouble yet to come, when he imagines the day his parents met. He imagines himself standing in a theater, watching a film of his parents on a date. In his mind's eye, he speaks directly to the screen.

> I'm not the type of person to make a scene, but if I were, I suppose now would be as good a time as any to stand up and not yell, but interrupt as politely as possible, say "Excuse me, I'm not saying you shouldn't get married, because I think it's not a bad idea. Still, I think there are issues here between the two of you that need to be explored."

When we spoke about why he used this technique, Hemley speculated, "don't we all, in memoir, want to be able to go back and say 'no, don't do that'?"

Taking a Tip from Screenwriters

The screenwriter's technique for mapping out a plot is called a "beat sheet." For a screenwriter, a beat is a place of action in the story, a point where the action changes. A beat sheet is another kind of map, a way for the author to keep tabs on how her plot moves forward in an organized and coherent way.

While some writers may use a computer spreadsheet, sticky notes, or pages of notebook paper, I've stolen a page (so to speak) from screenwriters, and keep my "beats" on index cards.

TIP: Try using 5×7 index cards to jot down summaries of each of your scenes and the character interactions in them. These can be as simple as "alone in kitchen eating chili during party in living room," indicating the action and characters in that scene. As scenes accrue in your manuscript, periodically transfer just the short summaries to cards. Arrange the cards with pushpins on a bulletin board or a piece of foam core. Index cards held in place with pins are easy to move around. Moving them around frees you from worrying about the final structure as you write. When you want to, you can take what you originally thought would be the perfect second scene and try it out as the third, or the seventh, until you have a story flowing in a way that feels natural and right. Then, go back to your manuscript and restructure it following the milestones you've created using the index cards.

Neil White found his middle for his prison memoir *In The Sanctuary of Outcasts* through what he calls trial and error. He explained to me that "the longest chapter is six or seven pages, but there is physical movement. The protagonist and characters in different physical settings creates a sense that time has passed."

His memoir is divided by dates that span his time in prison, with eighty short chapters under headings that begin the book with "PART I, My First Day, May 3, 1993" and end the book with "PART VI, My Last Day, April 25,1994." Within that structure, chapters open at different locations in the prison, such as the visiting room, another prisoner's room, a walk around the prison grounds, or in the cafeteria.

Write What You Don't Know

Fiction writers have license to make up what their characters do and say, but memoir isn't fiction. (A few Internet searches for "falsified memoir" will bring up plenty of news stories about authors who made up all or parts of what were ostensibly memoirs.) The temptation is there with every dead end, but nonfiction authors have an implicit contract with their readers (and a legal contract with their publishers) to be honest.

But writing what you don't know is an essential part of grief memoir. The concept can seem frustrating: not knowing exposes you as an author to the uncertainty of writing about real life. Your memories are imperfect, and you may find that what you believed were fact are flawed, too. In grief, memories are suspect, broken, or inaccessible. There are so many things you *do* know about your grief, but what you don't know—and the possibility that you may never know—is an essential part of your story, too. Writing what you don't know can be a place where flights of fancy, conjecture, and imagination come into play.

At a writers' workshop where I led a memoir class, a woman asked a question that generated a ripple of agreement among the dozen or so writers gathered around the big table in a church social hall. She had begun a memoir about her marriage, but her writing stalled when she recognized that she didn't know the truth about a story from her husband's background. Her husband didn't know either, and the relatives involved were either deceased or claimed that they weren't aware of the story. The missing information that kept her from moving ahead in her writing was a family tale about a mysterious romance in a European country in a long-ago war.

Did it happen, the woman wondered aloud. How can I find out for sure, she asked, if there are no records, no witnesses, and so much time has passed? Why, she fretted, did no one think to write it down for her to find so many years and countries later?

I told her that she could try looking at this detour in a different way. The absence of ship's manifests, photographs, love letters, and only a vague tale that's become mythic *is* the story element she's looking for.

A memoir is different from an exhaustive family history. Some memoirs do include genealogy charts or maps, and many include photographs, but memoir is the author's story. "Memoir" comes from the Latin word *memor*—the same root as memorial, remembrance, and memory. The Latin word means "to remember." But memory is imperfect. Rather than being angry or feeling another loss in the absence of the information you had hoped to use, look at how you can write about the things that you don't know. Not knowing doesn't mean that you write a partial story. Instead, the things you did to look for the missing information and how you felt when you found it—or never found it—is an essential part of your plot.

Writing what you don't know doesn't mean leaving blank spaces in the plot or on the page. The path in your memoir might be pockmarked with these land mines, and for fear of stepping on one, you'll stop writing. How can you move forward if you don't know what really happened between two people on one day during the Second World War? How can you write your memoir if you don't remember your father's actual last words to you?

MY STORY:

My father would be seventy-eight now if he hadn't died a week after his sixty-fifth birthday. I grieve that he did not live to be old. I grieve the lost opportunity of moments between us that had not yet happened. We were learning to be a better father and daughter to one another, and I was beginning to spend nonthreatening time with a man I had known mostly as volatile. This grief is my actively patching over his broken places, and wishing he could have been the man that I would rather he had been. He may have wanted to be that man, too. I can't know this now.

My father was well cared for by hospice in the last months of his illness. He died in his home, in a hospital bed in his living room. He died in the middle of the night. I know this because his wife called me to tell me that he had died. Her call woke me. I had known that this would be his last night, and knew, too, that he was more comfortable knowing that I was a thousand miles away, at home with my husband. My father and I had spoken early that evening, his wife holding the phone to his mouth in what I knew from my visits was a pleasant room with a crocheted afghan, a hanging plant in the window, and a video tape player and television on a rolling cart near the fireplace. My father breathed with the harsh Cheyne-Stokes gasps, the sound of his body working hard, like the sound of a handsaw rasping against a log. What had once been his booming voice had become soft, as if he were already receding down a tunnel.

Telling him that I loved him was difficult. This was new territory for us, words I hadn't said to my father since I was young enough to be tucked into bed. I told him that it was okay to go, although the words seemed to me like lines I had practiced. They came honestly. I meant them. I had not rehearsed what I would say, or even let myself wonder if I would get the chance to speak to him as he died. I had imagined my father's death coming as a surprise, an event for which I could not prepare.

I comforted my father on the phone. He didn't have the energy to speak more than a few words. As I listened to him breathe, I felt helpless in our estrangement for the first time, and wished that our tentative reconnection had started sooner so that we would not be nine states apart at the hour of his death. I could not get to him in time, and I wasn't sure that any good would come for either of us if I panicked. The thing I wanted most, there in my kitchen in boxer shorts and a T-shirt, lit only by the nightlight beside the sink and the greenish glow from the wall phone, was for my father to feel no pain and, for what might be the first time in his life, no anxiety. There was nothing he could do now, nothing his wife or hospice care or I could do that would stop what was happening. I imagined his dog with him on the bed, and I crossed my fingers in hope that she was calm at the sounds of her master's distress.

I told my father something I hadn't planned to. I hadn't known how this moment would feel until I was in it, and the words came out, as if I were the parent and he the child.

I told him what I wanted to tell myself.

"Don't be scared," I said.

My father's breathing rattled and shook, and I felt him waiting, drawing reserves.

And here my memory goes blank. I don't remember what he said. A movie script would have him saying "I love you." He might have. He probably did. I probably said it back. I remember a queasy sense of finality as I put the phone back in the cradle, and going back to bed where my husband was waiting, and crying for a very few minutes before I went to sleep.

What I don't remember about loss has a place in my story. Absence of information gives the writer a place to step back and consider on the page why the character, in this case, myself, forgets information. No one remembers everything, or goes through life taking notes or listening with an earpiece as if they're in a police drama. Sometimes what we want to research doesn't exist in public or personal archives. For all the journal-keeping that writers do, life itself takes precedence over in-the-moment recording.

I don't remember my father's last words to me because my emotions were running high in those moments in a rush of love and grief and anger and resolve. The best that I could do for both of us was be with him as a daughter. I knew in those few minutes that I didn't want to divert my attention from my father. A pad of paper and a jar of pens are always by our phone—I could have written as he spoke—but in this conscious moment of deep loss, I chose to be a daughter first and a writer second.

Natasha Trethewey, a Pulitzer Prize—winning poet and the nineteenth Poet Laureate of the United States, writes in her memoir, *Beyond Katrina: A Meditation on the Mississippi Gulf Coast* about how the position of not knowing can lead to discovery. In this selection from a scene about sorting through her grand-parents' lives in segregated North Gulfport, Mississippi, she writes,

> Stacks of quitclaim deeds in a strongbox in the family safe show Son Dixon's acquisition of large corner lots on major thoroughfares in North Gulfport—the intersections of old Highway 49 and a street now named Martin Luther King, Jr., Boulevard; MLK and Alabama Avenue; MLK and Arkansas—and other properties on Florida or backed up to new Highway 9. The dates on the deeds, the calendar from Leretta's beauty shop, the early Eisenhower for President button—who knows why it was saved?—all hint at a story of 1950s Gulfport.

"I love that part of writing," Trethewey said, when I asked her about this piece. "What is undiscoverable but knowable because of speculation around the parts we do know opens avenues about what could have happened." In the passage above, she sees the deeds in a strongbox in the family safe, and can identify the property locations, the dates of the transactions, and a souvenir from her grandmother's business. It's the presence of a political button among the financial records that raises questions. The reason for someone having placed it among the family records can never be clear; those people are gone.

"It's the parts we don't know, the mysterious parts, that are for a creative writer the most exciting," she told me. Trethewey's inclusion of the phrase, "who knows why it was saved?" makes her a foreground character in the scene, one who is unsure, and thinking almost aloud. Trethewey calls this "letting the seams show." The reader is made aware of the author as a character in her own true story as she wonders about this box of family records. Showing herself not knowing helps Trethewey communicate that *Beyond Katrina* is "about memory and forgetting."

Endings, or "Yes, and . . ."

I was talking to friend at a party about the ending he had just written for his film. His protagonist, a little boy, meets his masked hero at last, but he's sorely disappointed. The hero isn't the idol he had convinced himself he would find, and after working for almost the entire plot to have his troublesome nerdiness redeemed by proximity to his hero, the little boy is at a loss.

"So that's not really the end," the screenwriter said.

"Yes," I said to the screenwriter. It was a statement, not a question.

"Yes," he agreed.

And together we said, "Yes, and . . ."

An ending isn't the moment when you run out of writing steam. A satisfying ending begins with that moment of "yes, and" in your plot. In my friend's screenplay, the ending will have to be not that the boy finds his hero, but that the boy begins to change on his own as a result of his efforts to meet his hero. It's up to you to find where the story you are writing should end. How have you changed and moved forward in your life?

The "yes, and" for my story is that, yes my sisters died, and I learned to find my voice without them. In her memoir, *Here if You Need Me*, Kate Braestrup weathers the death of her husband, a Maine State Trooper, in a car accident. A widowed mother of four, Braestrup attends divinity school and becomes a minister, the profession her husband had intended to pursue as his own second career. The "yes, and" in her memoir can be seen as "yes" her husband was killed, "and" Braestrup became a chaplain in the Maine Warden Service, helping with search and rescue missions in the wilderness. For you as a writer, the idea of "yes, and" marks the place on your plot map where the renewal for the protagonist—you—starts to become clear.

Another way to phrase this could be "yes, but," although I prefer "and." "And" has a more positive, forward-moving feeling. It's not a contradiction, but a continuation. Your memoir's existence proves that you have survived to tell the tale. A well-made ending is a new beginning. In a memoir of grief and loss, it's that place on the page when the you, as the author—and when the reader—is satisfied that the protagonist telling the story can make it from here. A good ending fulfills an implicit promise made in the beginning, whether it's to tell how the survival occurred, or how the you (the protagonist) has grown as a result of the loss. Perhaps revisiting the "occasion of the telling" becomes the ending to your memoir, like a circle closing as the story comes to a close.

John Gunther writes in the "Aftermath" of *Death Be Not Proud*:

When Johnny died, nature took note.

He writes of a storm, but he also shows that life in its essence—nature, weather, emotion—continues vividly during his seventeen-year-old son's funeral. It's his own version of "yes, and."

Agents and editors sometimes call this technique "reader reward." That's the sense the reader gets that there will be an emotional reward or feeling of satisfaction after spending time with your story. It's "writer reward," too. In choosing to take up the task of telling your story of grief, you've acknowledged that you have survived to write it, but that alone may not be a compelling enough reason to let others know what happened. Now that you are a survivor, you are changed. Who are you now, and how did you get here?

No writer or reader wants a sparkling, disingenuous ending that wipes the slate clean of grief. A generic story with the emotional authority of a smiley-face sticker would not only be false, but a grave injustice to your story and hard work. That said, a writer doesn't want to double back and end his memoir where he began it, in a place of deep grief. The plot of your memoir is the story of your coming to some understanding about your loss and how you will move forward.

Author Darin Strauss writes about this delicate balance toward the end of *Half a Life,* in the passage:

> Things don't go away. They become you. There is no end, as T. S. Eliot somewhere says, but addition: the trailing consequence of further days and hours. No freedom from the past, or from the future.

"We don't close the book" of our lives, Strauss explained when I asked him about these lines. "We allow ourselves to add other chapters, to integrate this one dark chapter into the rest of our stories."

Marianne Leone writes of her similar outlook in the last chapter of *Knowing Jesse.*

> Jesse is present, found, invoked by giving. To be present in the world, the world without Jesse, that's the hardest thing. But it's the only way to find him.

TIP: You can begin to locate where your ending begins in your memoir by placing a virtual pin in your map of the memoir's narrative, locating a place in your story that marks where you have come to understand what your story of grief means to you as a survivor that brings you to the "yes, and."

Why an Honest Ending Is a New Beginning

A well-written, honest ending is a resonant ending. You know from living and writing about your own grief and in reading about others' losses that nothing is wrapped up with a neat bow.

A resonant ending echoes in the reader's heart and mind. Because the reader has invested herself in the character—you— she wants to know that the character's story will go on. The character and the reader both move forward in their lives. Not everything in an honestly told story can be solved happily. However, a satisfactory ending hints at a new beginning for at least one of the characters, namely, the writer.

The reader has come to know the incident of loss. As she comes to the end of the memoir, she wants to know that as changed as the characters are, the world keeps turning, and the protagonist or his family has made it, for better or worse, past the immediate hazard of their trials.

MY STORY:

I was sure that I knew how my memoir would begin and end. It would begin with my parents' wedding, and two hundred and some pages later, end with my own. I saw this as a technique I could use to complete the memoir using a circle that connected the very different images of their wedding and mine. I was wrong.

My editor called me after she read the manuscript, and one of the first things she said was, "you know that's not the ending, right?"

I was curious and a little afraid to dig deeper into my story, and myself, to find what she envisioned as the best ending. My wedding wasn't it. The ending I'd written was too obvious: a neatly prepared path that I had arranged to guide my tumultuous story.

In the months that followed, I worked hard to figure out what the "right" ending would be. I interrogated the work, as the academics say, reading and rereading to find clues in my own text to how my story ended. As a memoirist, I couldn't, and wouldn't, contrive an ending. If this had happened or that had turned out another way, what a great ending I would have. But this hadn't happened and that hadn't turned out a different way.

I lay the chapters as printed pages along the hallway in my house, stretching from the front door past the kitchen and the den and up to the second floor. I walked among the stacks of pages, moving part of a chapter to the middle of another, and so forth, trying to force the ending to emerge. I felt like I was driving in heavy snow again, peering out my window for a glimpse of the yellow line. I was angry at myself for creating an ending for the memoir that didn't work, and angry at my story for so reliably presenting difficulty in my life. I couldn't even finish my own memoir without anger and depression.

I tried writing various endings, but was sure I'd written all that I wanted to say. But sometime during the writing and revision process, the beginning of the memoir was no longer my parents' wedding, which was now a few chapters in. The beginning was now a section about my own contemplation of the losses that come with passage of time.

And looking anew at that beginning, I found my ending. I closed the circle using the substantive story. The memoir ends with a flashback of me as a teenager writing in my journal, commenting to myself about the passage of time.

Katharine Weber's memoir ends in water, as it begins. She concludes *The Memory of All That* with a scene in which she, now married and the mother of two, empties her grandmother's ashes into the sea. After inviting the reader to "wade in" with her as a toddler in her father's arms in the beginning of the book, ending the memoir with a scene in water felt emotionally satisfying and structurally right. Weber explained to me when I asked her about the ending that "it seems so resolved, there with my grandmother whose loving spirit was a such a rescue for me."

As a writer, Rebecca McClanahan resists the word "ending." Because a well-crafted ending brings the reader (and the writer) to the sense of a possible new beginning, McClanahan says she's started calling endings "openings."

Abigail Thomas's memoir *A Three Dog Life* ends with a scene in which she visits her husband, who has a traumatic brain injury, at the rehabilitation center where he lives. For the first time, they talk about the accident that caused his injury. Thomas realizes that her husband is trying to remember what she wants to forget. She concludes the memoir this way:

> A minute goes by. I ask Rich if he knows how long we've been married.
>
> "About a year," he answers.
>
> I shake my head. "Seventeen years," I say, "we got married in 1988 and it's 2005."
>
> "Abby," he says, smiling, "our life has been so easy that the days glide by."

"It was so moving," she says of that conversation. "His reality at that moment was so different from my own version of reality, it drew me up short. I loved the contrast of what he had been through with the moment he was in, and if felt almost as if with those few words he had made it my reality, too."

The best stories stay with the reader long after the last page is turned. The characters feel genuine, and the reader has followed their story and held it close to her heart. Triumphs and failures captured on the page thrum in the readers' mind even after the book is returned to the shelf. This is resonance, the "yes, and." It's what makes a memoir unforgettable.

Writing through grief carries strong emotions, including anger, into your story, but they often belong there. It's gratifying to the reader—and that includes you as you read your own work—to witness the author's genuine, honest feelings at work.

THE NEXT STEP

1. What kind of person are you? Are you someone who forgets his keys? Tosses fast-food wrappers in the backseat of his car? Can you tell a joke well, or do you always forget the punch line? Author Ethan Gilsdorf suggests listing the expressions you find yourself saying aloud (in my case, a particularly pithy swear from one of my favorite books that I can't print here), your nervous gestures (I bite my lower lip), and things you know about through what Gilsdorf calls "accidental expertise" (I'm pretty good at understanding medical terminology). How do these traits shape your character on the page? Do they trigger scene ideas? Expand one of those short descriptions into a scene, making sure that a trait of yours moves the plot forward in some way.

2. Make a list of five traits that you consider negative in the person or place that you are grieving. These can be as simple as "popped gum" or "never remembered other people's names," or "the water there smelled like a wet dog." Write a descriptive paragraph in which these traits are demonstrated by the character or place.

3. In order to work your way even more deeply into your material, write a sensory description of the "occasion of the telling." Use as many senses (taste, smell, touch, sight, and sound) as you can. Stretch yourself a little. What does fear taste like? For me, it's metal foil. A student once told me that fear tasted to him like celery. What does cold air feel like on your bare shoulders? How does a ringing phone sound when it's across the house and you're afraid there's bad news?

4. Write a scene about something that gives you shame, pain, or sorrow in your story, but don't refer to yourself

by name or by the personal pronoun "I"—instead, use "he" or "she" as appropriate. Now replace that pronoun ("he" or "she") with the pronoun "I." Notice if this change in voice on the page makes you anxious or want to deflect any of the story. Are you comfortable with the first-person voice in the deepest parts of your grief memoir?

5. Nineteenth-century author Henry James wrote, "A writer is someone upon whom nothing is lost." While Henry James didn't hang out in coffee shops or ride the subway, it's likely that he listened carefully to the interactions in the world around him. Sharpen your own observational skills by listening, in a noninvasive way, to mundane conversations that occur around you in public. Avoid the temptation to write down what you hear the moment you hear it. Instead, build your ability to write how real people speak by remembering phrases from real conversations. Don't write what you've overheard until after you leave the coffee shop, subway, or elevator. As you notice the rhythms of people's speech, their different styles of slang, and how individuals communicate different emotions in various settings, you'll find that writing dialogue becomes increasingly more fluid.

6. Identify a section in a memoir that you admire. Notice how sentences are constructed, if they are long or short or both, how action and description are paced, and how often direct dialogue is used. Just for fun, write a few paragraphs of your memoir's draft in that same style, or conversely, rewrite the passage you're reading the way you would have written it. As you read other memoirs, remember that I'm not advocating plagiarism. You wouldn't copy another writer's material and claim it as your own. But you can read, listen, and in your own writing get a feeling for the rhythm and shading of a writer whose skill you admire. And then you tell your own story.

7. A blank page can be intimidating, particularly when you have a complicated or difficult story to tell. Combine that with the rarity of an uninterrupted day to write, and sometimes not much gets done. One way to conquer the blank-page horrors and the 'I don't have time to *really* write' constraint is to start where you are. You have time for one sentence a day. If you're at work, write that single sentence and email it to yourself. Katharine Weber suggests opening a separate email account for these messages. One sentence a day equals seven sentences a week. Regular emails to yourself about "here's an idea for the first chapter" and "I just remembered that the neighborhood kid who shot out our porch light with a BB gun was called A.J." will add up to material for a rough draft quicker than you might think.

8. Physical actions indicate behavior as much as or more than how a character speaks. Describe the physical actions of a close friend, family member, or colleague when he or she avoids a topic. What physical cues show denial in this character?

   What do they do with their hands?

   Where do they focus their gaze?

   What habits (throat clearing, knuckle cracking, or joking, for example) do they express?

   What's their favorite "topic changing" subject?

   What's their favorite "topic changing" activity?

9. Frame your story as a fairy tale. Start a page with the phrase "Once upon a time . . . ," and see what happens. You can play around with fantasy for this exercise, and change the setting or characters to fit your concept of a classic Brothers Grimm or Hans Christian Andersen setting. Who in your story of grief is the evil prince, the imperious king, or the ugly duckling?

10. Where did your loss take place? Your childhood home? On a trip to a place you'd never been before? A neighbor's yard, or a rain-slicked intersection? With some

blank pages and a pen or pencil, draw a map (a bad one's fine, it's only for you) of the place where grief entered your life. Continue this exercise by drawing other maps of routes taken in good times and in bad. See if these maps help answer the narrative prompt, "and then what?" in putting your plot together, or if they help you visualize places and times important to your memoir.

Three

BARGAINING

✦

YOUR MEMOIR'S FORM

When you write a grief memoir, you bargain with yourself
and with your material to negotiate the right form for the narrative. You assess your memories, what you've written in draft
and in your journals, and the research you have done and have
yet to do as you determine what belongs in the story, and what's
an unwelcome diversion or too emotionally difficult to revisit.
You also bargain with the people who appear on the page and
in your real life. Memoir isn't autobiography, which is a detailed, straightforward, self-written—sometimes ghostwritten—
account of an entire life. Instead, any well-written memoir is a
consciously, lyrically constructed examination of one or two
powerful events that have affected your life.

A memoir can take on many forms and still uphold the necessary plot structure of beginning, middle, and end. "How
many words *is* a book?" a woman asked me during the conversation at a bookstore after I'd read from my memoir. Her question sounded to me like a Zen koan, a riddle that can't be
answered logically. The answer is "as many words as it takes,"

but saying so might have made me sound like Gollum in *The Hobbit*.

Bargaining

Kübler-Ross's third stage of grief is called "Bargaining," when the person who is dying wants to try to negotiate with whomever they view as a higher power as the finality of death is approaching. They want to gain more time or find a way to compromise. But bargaining isn't limited to the dying. Culturally, we often bargain against trouble without even realizing that we're doing it. Parents and children bargain; good grades are rewarded, so are chores well done. In my case, I believed that if I took care to leave my sister Susie's bed undisturbed in our shared bedroom, that might bring her home from another hospitalization.

In the memoir, I wrote about my bargain this way:

> I went to bed and woke up in a bedroom that was only half-occupied. I imagined a painted line on the floor dividing our room in two, and offered a silent and general apology if I had to cross it to get to my closet or out the door.

As writers witnessing our own grief and trauma, and often our family's, too, we bargain with ourselves and with our story. We think that we'll write after old Uncle Leonard dies, because he might be angry if he reads this memoir. Maybe you bargain by telling yourself that you'll write the memoir when your kids are in college, or when you figure out exactly what you want to say, or when you get enough time off from work. If you are actively writing, you might bargain with yourself this way: when I finish a page, I'll go watch TV.

❈   ❈   ❈

When I was small, I was afraid to step on a crack, fearing for the well-being of my mother's back. I would start an entire sidewalk over if my saddle shoe went down on anything remotely like a split in the concrete. In the Deep South, where I live, the first breakfast of the New Year represents bargaining. Serving black-eyed peas and collard greens represents the hope for luck and money in the coming year. When I set a table, I make sure to turn the knives so that the blades face inward, toward the plate. If someone else sets the table, I try to casually turn the knives the "right" way without anyone catching me in the act. I'm fulfilling a superstitious ritual I learned from my mother: the knife blade out means someone will get hurt. If the knife blade's in, all will be well. I'm striking a bargain to make right what hasn't yet gone wrong.

Bargains like these are the kinds that writers make to forestall what we know will happen. We know that we will have to sit down at the desk and write. And writing, especially about our own grief, is a gut-wrenching, squirmy business. Until you're done. And then it's a victory.

Bargaining in your writing goes beyond making a deal with yourself and your demons. You've already agreed with yourself that you'll write. But that doesn't mean that the deals and trade-offs are over. They're waiting to be made within the work itself, in everything from the narrative form your memoir will take to the research you do and the choices you make about what material to use and what to set aside.

In this section, you'll explore the ways that your memoir's structure can create surprising additional impact, and we will experiment with different memoir styles. You will also delve into how research supports your memoir, and learn to locate and interpret everyday resources you didn't know you had. We'll look at ways that newspaper headlines, recipes, and even do-it-yourself field trips can inform your memoir, placing you and your very personal experience of loss in the context of the wider world. When you've done this, you've created a strong sense of place and community for you and your reader.

Commercial memoirs are traditionally written as straightforward prose. As the genre has expanded and grown in popularity, writers who have mastered the form have made inroads by writing all or parts of their memoirs in groundbreaking forms like lists, graphic novels, and even incorporating elements of fiction. For example, in *Companion to an Untold Story*, author Marcia Aldrich uses an alphabetized reference book style called a "companion" to structure her writing about a close friend's suicide and her reactions. Cartoonist Alison Bechdel's award-winning graphic memoir *Fun Home: A Family Tragicomic* tells, and shows, in her unadorned drawing style, the story of her childhood in the funeral home her parents operated, her father's death, and her coming out as a lesbian.

But before you envision your completed memoir taking these forms, imagine the small type on the television screen during a car commercial. This kind of stunt driving (or stunt writing) comes with the warning, "trained driver, closed road." For a writer new to memoir or a writer who hopes to see his memoir commercially published, techniques like these can be good experiments in finding story and exploring insights. Ultimately, though, it's the straightforward, first-person structure that usually appeals to the commercial market.

When a Few Words Are Enough

The shortest story of grief that I know is attributed to Ernest Hemingway, who is said to have written this single-sentence short story:

"For Sale: Baby Shoes, Never Worn."

There must be more to the telling, we say, but the emotional impact of this single abruptly worded sentence is undeniable. Why those shoes were never worn is left up to the reader. The author never explains why the shoes are for sale, or who's selling them. As writers who come to the page with our own stories of grief, we bring our own reflexive answers to the experience of reading Hemingway's bonsai tree of a story.

Perhaps it's this unforgettable one-line example of fiction that's given rise to the increasing popularity of six-word memoirs and the stylistic triumphs in "flash" fiction and nonfiction.

Hemingway's dramatic six-word story leaves much to the imagination. It can't reveal everything; it's constrained by the miniature form. But that miniscule story delivers an emotional punch that leaves the reader reeling, stamped with the image of those shoes. That impact is a lot like grief itself.

Your story doesn't have to be as miniature as Hemingway's. But how would your memoir work if you took risks with the length, the style, or even the way the text appears on the page? Sometimes an experimental or unusual form can give a memoir extra significance that reaches beyond words.

Here, Nick Flynn, in his memoir *Another Bullshit Night in Suck City*, writes about his father's alcoholism. Flynn uses an entire chapter to list synonyms for drunkenness, and his words come at us in an overwhelming torrent, disorienting the reader. At first glance, this chapter's four pages seem to be a clever writing trick, a way to boggle the reader's mind with myriad ways to talk about one thing. As we read, however, we realize that we are being shown the cycle of alcoholism almost from within. We're at the bar with this insistent person calling for a drink, and the apparently simple, short words and phrases that accrue relentlessly trap us there with the drinker. We are made drunk on words, spun around with the author's use of a multitude of vernacular descriptions of the speaker's descent from colloquial amity to inebriation, bitterness, regret, and drinking again.

The usual I say. Blood of Christ, I say. Essence. Spirit. Medicine. A hint. A taste. A bump. A snort. I say top shelf. Straight up. Two fingers. A shot. A sip. A nip. I say another round. I say brace yourself. Lift a few. Hoist a few. Work the elbow. Bottoms up. Belly up. Leg up. Set 'em up. Freshen up. What'll it be. Name your poison.

That is how the chapter begins. Here is how it ends.

Down the hatch I say. I wouldn't say no I say. I say whatever he's having. I say next one's on me. I say match you. I say bottoms up. Put it on my tab. I say one more. I say same again.

Flynn's incantatory rhythm throughout this entire chapter is designed to throw the reader off balance, reenacting the feeling of being drunk. When we talked, he suggested that the chapter be read aloud to fully experience the effect of a repetitive flow of words. The chapter has a chronology all its own, he says, that mimics the intensity of the speaker's drinking experience. The identity of the speaker—the "I" in this chapter—is left unspecified. "Some of the chapters are about [my father] or me," Flynn told me. "This one's deliberately unclear."

What bargains will you make with the form your memoir takes? What will you have to leave out, or write in, in order to make the form work? Nick Flynn's form in the section above is borrowed from a Native American genesis myth in which the world is spoken into being.

> TIP: A form or shape is the result of a bargain or negotiation: certain scenes, interactions, and moments have to take place in your memoir, but not others. One thing happens and another results. Take a look at the rituals that have been part of your experience of grief and grieving, and think about how your writing might mimic the ways that they are enacted.
>
> Imagine the AIDS Memorial Quilt displaying its tens of thousands of names. The quilt has toured the country for more than twenty years in public exhibitions created to remind visitors of the deaths from AIDS and HIV-related illness. The presence of the quilt itself has allowed visitors to grieve.

How would a quilt, or the way a quilt is made, serve the way you could shape a draft of your story? Another example is in the physical gestures of a woman who never fails to donate funds to an animal-rescue organization when a pet or friend's pet dies. The act of writing the check, folding and placing it in the envelope, the peeling of the stamp, and applying it to the envelope's corner don't undo the loss of an animal companion, but they're the precise, almost mechanistic movements that ease her sorrow, and on the receiving side, give care to a small creature. Is there a section of your memoir that could, in how it's written, mirror a set of step-by-step actions that attempt to alleviate the pain of loss?

In *Nola: A Memoir of Faith, Art, and Madness*, Robin Hemley combines pages of his sister's journal with his own narrative writing, his mother's editorial comments and scratch-outs on his sister's work, transcription excerpts from an audio tape of a session he had with a hypnotist, court documents, and drawings. The different documents are indicated by different typefaces, the drawings set apart by page placement and margins.

"Allowing everyone [in the family] his or her say, allowing truth in the space between contradictions [is] where the most profound truth lies," he told me. "The way people contradict each other and themselves is the key to understanding human behavior."

Another example of unusual form is Joan Wickersham's award-winning memoir of her father's suicide, *The Suicide Index: Putting My Father's Death in Order*. The book is organized as the title says: as an index, a method of cross-referencing information to try to make sense of her loss. Faith Adiele's award-winning memoir, *Meeting Faith: An Inward Odyssey* is the story of her experiences in Thailand as she becomes ordained as a Buddhist nun. Adiele, a biracial woman of color, writes in the memoir's preface that the book is about two taboo subjects in America—religion and race. This cultural memoir of faith is also a grief memoir in its own way: Adiele explained to me that writing the book was a reaction to her despondence about the racism and sexism she had experienced in her home country. The memoir looks unusual on the page, with text in the sidebars that she calls the "paratext": short sections near the margins that provide insight into Thai culture, Buddhist concepts, and the science of meditation that surrounded her life there as they surround the memoir on the page. She says that to her, the memoir's mix of blocks of text and white space on the page helped her convey the way she felt living on one daily meal, keeping a vow of silence, and trying to meditate nineteen hours a day. When I asked her about her memoir's structure, she explained that the memoir's main narrative moves backward in time and deeper into her personal history in a way that's similar to the inward feeling that a meditation practice provides. Adiele also uses photographs, drawings, and charts in her memoir to engage readers, regardless of their own spiritual choices.

What's in your story and how you choose to write it might suggest a form to try in your drafts, if you keep an eye out for the hints your story's giving you. Explore. Experiment. Try a form on for size, and if the style doesn't suit the story, try something else. Of course, as Nick Flynn points out, your material may need a plain-spoken style. "You don't have to have fireworks with every piece," he says.

When Chronology Matters

The most obvious way to tell a story is in chronological order, following the natural order of time. (The word "chronological" comes from the Greek word *kronos,* or time.) Strict chronology, however, isn't necessarily the first choice for organizing a memoir. Telling a section of your story in the order that time passed is an excellent method for assembling complicated elements that could confuse a reader (or you, as you sort through them). An example could be a series of actions that escalate over a period of time, such as the build-up to a military troop movement, the tense minutes in a boardroom before an executive decision that will change lives, or the days that passed as you stayed in a hotel, practicing in a mirror how you would tell your husband you were leaving him for good.

Telling a story out of chronological order is called "a-chron-ological," the "a" prefix meaning "absence of" or "without." This is nonlinear storytelling. But nonlinear storytelling isn't randomized storytelling. Your memoir may start organically with a scene that depicts why you decided to write, or with a scene that depicts an interaction after your loss has taken place. Memoir comes strongly from memory, and memory isn't linear. Memory can be triggered by something as common as a song lyric or the view from an airplane window.

Marianne Leone wanted *Knowing Jesse* to be told in a nonlinear format to mimic her belief that "grief is a sniper" that attacks in random moments. However, a distinct focus in her memoir is her struggle to make sure that Jesse received the quality of education that he deserved. The plot element of Jesse's school experiences and Marianne's efforts to ensure that they did justice to her son's intellect rather than his physical disability, create part of the plot map for the memoir. "That was the only linear part of the book," she says. The memoir begins on the first anniversary of Jesse's death, and moves through time not in strict adherence to the chronology of Jesse's life, but in chapters that also address Leone's memory, dreams, and the writing of the book itself.

Another example is Dorothy Gallagher's memoir *How I Came into My Inheritance: And Other True Stories*, which begins with Gallagher's retelling her experience placing her elderly mother in a nursing home after she suffers a broken hip. There's more to the story as it continues: Gallagher's descriptions of her father's obstinacy, decline, and death, and her unsentimental memories that move back and forth over time. She recalls what she knows about her family in Stalinist Russia, the McCarthy-era United States, and herself in modern-day New York. Each of these, out of order, work together to connect her memoir as a whole, a story of inheriting the legacy of a family.

Bargaining with the Mail

A memoir in letters is "epistolary," composed all or in large part of epistles, or letters. Epistolary applies to email correspondence, too. A cache of family correspondence that shines in its language and period references or captures a lost loved one's way of speaking might be calling out to be used in the form you received it—as letters. But your memoir probably can't be told entirely in correspondence. The reader needs to know why you hold these letters in high enough regard to use them in their original form, and what role they play in helping you tell your story. However, a back and forth volley between characters that enlivens your description of their time, place, and state of mind, or that narrates loss in a short series of letters or postcards can connect sections in your memoir, add depth, and introduce new voices.

If you use letters, this is where "you the author" politely asks "you the grieving person" to step aside in order to evaluate with as little emotion as possible the ways that the letters, as letters, support the story. Every letter may matter a great deal to you, but they will matter less to your reader. Only the particularly resonant, funny, or poignant letters may work. Even the best letters may only work as excerpts. Try using short selections from the letters as section breaks in your writing or as chapter headings. Make use of the most effective elements of what they say and how they say it.

Rebecca McClanahan does this with lyrics, using words to the folk song "The Riddle Song" (also called "I Gave My Love a Cherry") to introduce sections of her novella-length essay "The Riddle Song: A Twelve-Part Lullaby."

McClanahan had difficulty finding the right form for the

work, partly because, as she explained to me, there are so many time periods covered in the piece. The essay is about childbirth and child bearing, mothering and not becoming a mother, which "I'd been writing about . . . for years," she says. Even though she'd rewritten the essay a variety of different ways, including trying it out as a three-hundred-page novel, she knew that something was still missing.

Driving home from a reading, McClanahan, tired, sang to keep herself awake. When she started singing "The Riddle Song" she realized she'd hit on the structure.

She told me that she "got home, got out scissors and glue and got out the essay and started cutting it up into pieces." Hearing the lyrics as she sang, she realized that the essay was "thematic, not chronological." Those themes were "babies, dead babies, [and] love." She writes:

> I gave my love a cherry that had no stone
>> Holly enters the room, panting. "Sorry I'm late," she says between gasps. "I wanted a good uterus to show you." Holly is always misplacing her visual aids. She plops down into the only remaining seat in the room, a bright orange beanbag. "Have you all been practicing? Remember, breathing is everything." Gasp. "July will be here before you know it." Beside me, my sister giggles.

In this example, you can start to see how each part of her twelve-part memoiristic essay begins with a lyric from this wistful song. Here, she makes a sudden transition into an active, almost frantic scene with a powerful sense of immediacy. Placed together, those two elements create a tonal contrast that pulls the reader into the narrative. They also begin to inform you, as a reader, about the author's voice and how she will guide you through this true story: strong emotion leavened with scene ("enters the room, panting"), humor ("a good uterus to show you"), the subject matter (pregnancy) and forward motion.

The next section, several pages later, begins:

I gave my love a chicken that had no bone

A female chick is born complete—thousands of ova in her left ovary—and her fate is determined by how well she uses her potential. A good layer can produce an egg a day and is prized for this ability, saved from the fate of her less fertile sisters who will end up in Sunday's roasting pan.

This section is about so much more than chickens. Consider the words "complete," "fate," and "potential," as well as the idea that infertility can cost someone—in the nominal sense, a chicken, in the substantive sense, a woman—if not her life, at least the perception of how well she can "produce."

The author's own "accidental expertise"—she frequently visited her grandparents' Indiana farm—comes into play, too, in her knowledge of hens and their reproductive systems, expertise that she uses as a tool to build the essay.

A collision like this of two elements in memoir or in essay are crucial to building plot and structure. McClanahan elaborated, telling me, "You can't start a fire with one stick. You've got to have two things rubbing together. The 'what happened to me' is only one stick. The other is form, or language, style, voice. . . . The conflict doesn't have to be in what happens. It can be created through form, design, and tone."

Writers should remember this important note on lyrics. Bear in mind as you write that using lyrics in your memoir can quickly make your very personal story devolve into a collection of words written by someone else. Certain lyrics may have significance for you, but they're unlikely to have the exact same resonance to your reader. Song lyrics are also usually owned by the songwriter or his or her music publisher, which can turn into a costly and time-consuming venture for you if you choose to publish your memoir. (Even "Happy Birthday to You" is protected by copyright.) Agents and editors tend to turn away from memoirs that rely too heavily on lyrics to tell their story, because the author hasn't done the work of using his or her own voice.

Alternating Chapters

In her memoir *Ecology of a Cracker Childhood*, naturalist Janisse Ray alternates chapters about growing up in a junkyard in South Georgia with chapters about the endangered longleaf pine forest, braiding her own story with that of the landscape that defines her.

The first chapter, "Child of Pine" opens with her parents searching for something that Ray at first doesn't name. In the pinewoods outside the junkyard they operated, they find a baby. Ray, of course, wasn't found in the woods, but born as any child is, and in this first chapter she gives the reader the creation story she was told about herself and her siblings.

> My sister had been found in a big cabbage in the garden; a year after me, my brother was discovered under the grapevine, and a year after that, my little brother appeared beside a huckleberry bush.

Writing this way, she establishes a sense of myth and wonder, as well as the importance of the natural world in her family's life.

The chapter after this one, "Below the Fall Line," opens with her explanation of the term "fall line," an invisible line running northeast across the state of Georgia separating the coastal plain from the Piedmont region. She continues:

> Ninety-eight percent of the presettlement longleaf pine barrens in the southeastern coastal plains were lost by 1986 . . . Natural stands—meaning not planted—have been reduced by about 99 percent.
>
> Apocalyptic.
>
> This was not a loss I knew as a child. *Longleaf* was a word I never heard. But it is a loss that as an adult shadows every step I take.

By alternating the focus of her chapters, Ray creates a parallel between protagonist and place. As the chapters accrue, you begin to understand on both a visceral and intellectual level how the person and place merge.

Stream of Consciousness

Stream of consciousness writing is less a form than a stylistic approach, and it's a daring and difficult feat for a writer sustaining a successful book-length narrative. Since stream of consciousness can read like a dream or a drug experience, if these are part of your story, why not try a few short sections written this way to put yourself in the frame of mind as you write your draft?

C. S. Lewis's *A Grief Observed* is a short memoir in stream of consciousness style, composed from the author's notebooks in which he recorded his thoughts about his wife's death, his life without her, and the questions he posed to his faith while grieving. Some paragraphs are only a sentence long. In his memoir, he directly addresses himself and his late wife, whom he refers to as "H," and ponders how to speak about death to his children and to strangers. An academic and a lay theologian, he also evaluates his perceptions of God.

Another example is Dave Eggers's memoir *A Heartbreaking Work of Staggering Genius*, in which he recounts his efforts to raise his younger brother after the deaths of both parents within a month of one another. Eggers employs stream of consciousness as well as fictional fantasy sequences to tell his wrenching story of loss.

> **TIP:** Try using an ongoing verbal and internal argument with yourself, your journal entries, or snippets from others' diaries and letters, and the loosely gathered elements of your story as you grieve to guide a stream of consciousness approach to your creativity in your journals, brain-sparks, and narrative drafts.

Metaphor

Imagery is the connective tissue of the nonlinear story. Selecting your most important imagery is another bargain you make: if you're writing a memoir that expands and contracts, or moves backward and forward as you tell your story, it's the strength of the metaphors you choose and the language of that imagery that binds those pieces together.

In this passage from Vladimir Nabokov's classic memoir, *Speak, Memory*, his mother, father, a host of servants, and a dachshund travel on a train in 1909, when he is about ten years old. With his mother, Nabokov plays a card game.

> In April of that year, Peary had reached the North Pole. In May, Shalyapin had sung in Paris. In June, bothered by rumors of new and better Zeppelins, the United States War Department had told reporters of plans for an aerial Navy.... At a collapsible table, my mother and I played a card game called durachki.

Young Vladimir isn't specifically aware of each advancement and change in the world around him—children don't tend to avidly keep up with world news—but the shadow of war on the horizon, which factors strongly in the memoir as it progresses, gives an ominous mood to what appears on the surface to be a scene about a boy and his mother whiling away the time.

Nabokov the adult writer gives the reader a look at the world he inhabited as a child, even though his character isn't yet fully aware of that world. Take a closer look at the imagery he's used in this scene to convey that idea: a boy looking only at what's directly in front of him (the card game) instead of looking out the window, where the landscape is in rapid motion. The table is collapsible, as is the stability of the world he knows. As we read, we know that playing cards can be shuffled, reordered, and moved. The cards, the train, and the table itself were real, and we know that from them he has created metaphor.

Metaphor can apply to how you view your writing process, too. "That search for meaning takes a long time," Neil White told me. Of a woman in the leprosarium with whom he became friends, he observed that, "Ella had been in her wheelchair for fifty years and had never gotten it right. She went straight for a while, veered off, hit a wall . . . watching Ella was a perfect metaphor for my process."

TIP: Take a close look at your drafts, journals, and your brain-sparks. Can you start to identify the images that consistently show up as you write about your loss? They're the building blocks of metaphor that will be the strongest in your writing, the images that matter to you personally and connect your unique memories and perspective with what has happened to you during times grief and in times of happiness. Recognizing and using your own set of images makes your writing as personal as a fingerprint.

Read through your work so far and make a list of descriptive images that you've used more than once. Circle words that come up often, and be alert to the ways you've described color, place, emotion, food, or anything that has strong meaning to you. You're beginning your collection of images that matter to you and your writing. If your drafts are already on a computer, most programs have a "find" feature. Try using it to see how often a word like "dream" or "dessert" or "home" or "forest"—whatever might be consistent for you—show up. Like a child's game book with a connect-the-dots puzzle, you've begun to find the metaphors that suit you best. One or two extended metaphors in your memoir will hold the work together very nicely. Too many metaphors and you've oversalted the soup. (See what I mean? "Puzzle" and "soup" aren't consistent images.)

Dreams, Signs, and Other Details That Can Add Meaning

You may also find that a sound or image that recurs in your dreams helps fuse your memoir into a unified whole. Marianne Leone's writing and imagery is often influenced by her dreams. When we talked about her use of dreams in *Knowing Jesse: A Mother's Story of Grief, Grace, and Everyday Bliss*, she advised writers to examine their dreams. Dreams only work in writing, she said, "if you draw the synchronicity to your waking life." Do the work of making the subconscious connection between what your dreaming mind sees and what can be written clearly in the memoir to convey your thoughts and feelings about your grief.

She begins her memoir with a dream.

All summer and fall I had been troubled by a dream I couldn't interpret. My mother, who had died that spring, appeared as a silent sentinel dressed in white, seated next to a café table covered by snowy linen on which one small candle burned. . . . The candle tipped over and fell behind the table. I reached for it and the candle disappeared, falling through a hole in the floor that magically revealed the candle lighting millions of others.

Later in the chapter, she writes,

The dream finally made sense on the morning of January 3, 2005, when I went to wake up my son for school and found him dead in his bed.

A few paragraphs later, she connects the images.

My son was wearing his T-shirt that read "Anime fiammagente"—souls aflame.

Leone doesn't present this dream on its own without context, which might have left the reader without a clear sense of how the material fits into the story. Instead, she explains the silent sentinel's appearance in a dream that she can't interpret. As readers, we want the author to connect the dream with her waking life and what's on her mind. Leone meets that need as she tells us why and how the dream came to make sense to her.

Author Robin Hemley told me that "anyone writing a book with any depth at all will have really weird dreams, because they're opening things that are pretty securely locked." Toward the end of his memoir, *Nola: A Memoir of Faith, Art, and Madness*, he writes about a dream that helped him visualize his inquiry into his sister's life and death, his relationship to her, and his family.

> I dream of words, round and crystalline, like fortune-teller balls, descending slowly through the depths of an ocean, and coming to rest gently on the bottom without shattering. . . . I felt peaceful, serene . . . I felt somehow reassured that the words had finally touched bottom.

His dream signifies to him that he's telling the story the way he should.

MY STORY:

My memoir *Invisible Sisters* breaks an unofficial rule and starts with a daydream: a state of reverie in which my sisters are alive and we three are grown, married, and parents of children splashing in a swimming pool. I had this dream and variations on it so often that I felt as if there were almost a parallel world where our lives had continued together. Allowing myself to wander there when I wrote felt like touching base with an alternate universe. It's what the Superman comics called Bizarro

World, but it was comforting and knowable, and it eased my heart.

Dreams are a recurring thread in my memoir, because as I wrote the book, I regularly had vivid dreams about my sisters. Because I was thinking about my sisters and our relationship almost constantly as I wrote, my sisters and the physical details of our lives were prominent in my mind. Not all the dreams were pleasant. Some were unsettling, others downright chilling.

Before Sarah died, I woke up one morning from a dream in which I'd tried to call her in to shore while she swam in the ocean. Her sensitivity to infection didn't allow her to swim in real life, and the sense I had in the dream was of uncomfortably letting her finally do whatever she chose.

> A voice whispered in my ear, telling me to let her go, that she knew what she was doing. I woke up weighted with awe, and called Sarah to tell her my dream. Sleepy, I dialed the wrong number, and then apologized to the stranger on the line. I didn't try again. Sarah would be on her way to work, I reasoned, no time to chat with me about my dreams.

I had this dream the night before Sarah died. The dream's significance became clear to me only after I started to examine my story. My dream foreshadowed what would become my task: learning to let my sister go.

Writing your dreams into a scene can change the pace and tone of the memoir for you and for the reader. A hallucinatory or realistic dream can counterbalance what is sometimes brutal reality. A nightmare or haunting dream can rend a dark hole in an otherwise placid scene. Dreams, handled deftly, can add richness and texture to your true story.

Much the same way that images in your dreams and in song lyrics can help guide you toward the substantive in your memoir, Natasha Trethewey finds meaning in a broken sign. Here, in a scene from her memoir *Beyond Katrina: A Meditation on the Mississippi Gulf Coast,* she arrives with her husband at the Mississippi church where her grandmother belonged and will be buried. Her brother will arrive in the company of police officers, who are escorting him from jail. The church is struggling to make repairs, years after the storm. Their insurance hasn't met their needs and membership has dwindled.

> On the ground level, windows on both sides of the church were boarded up, and a couple of the high windows up top that overlooked the balcony were still blown out. I could see birds flying in and out of them. The church marquis hadn't been repaired, and most of the glass was missing. A few letters hung on—an O on its side, what looked to be a broken F. Missing its smaller arm, it resembled the gallows in a child's game of hangman.

For a writer with grief on her mind, a broken sign is more than debris. "Hangman" is a child's game with an ominous provenance. The letters in the sign are themselves broken. For Trethewey, recognizing an image's potential begins with what she calls a "kind of photographic sensibility." She makes a picture in her head, she says, and allows her mind's eye to scan what's there. "A writer has to think photographically, to train herself to think that way." A writer has to learn to notice what matters to her.

Neil White, author of *In the Sanctuary of Outcasts,* believes in searching for meaning in every detail. "A writer won't always find it, but don't overlook anything," he says. "You've got to try ten or twelve things that don't work until you find what's spot-on."

Dreams may not be your way in to the images that guide your thinking. You may have photographs, letters, or documents that tie the pieces together. You may not know what your overarching images will be when you start writing. As you get more familiar with what your story means to you as a writer, the metaphors will show themselves.

Here is a paragraph from a student's work of fiction about a May–December romance. The younger woman is alone after her older lover's death. On the surface, the paragraph depicts the lover carving beautiful objects from food, but the use of metaphor in flowers and animals, delicate living things that bloom and fade, or arrive and depart soundlessly, introduces the transformation and change that the woman must accept.

> He cut her roses from tomatoes and thin, perfect butterflies from apple slices, etched swirling floral patterns into butternut squash and freed schools of cantaloupe fish from their thick-rind prisons. In his hands zucchini transformed into boats of green and white carnations and watermelons bloomed into crystalline lotuses dewy with liquid sugar; a daikon radish could morph into anything from a lily to a peacock, colorless and fine. He shaped beetroots into bloody purple camellias whose redness stained his hands for days afterward.

The author writes of squash, cantaloupe, zucchini, and watermelons, of carving and giving gifts, but with these images, she's created a metaphor about nourishment.

TIP: One cautionary note. You may fall deeply in love with the power of imagery and want to spend all your time with metaphor and its compatriots simile, analogy, symbolism, and so forth. Don't overload your memoir with conflicting images. When you find a very few that you like, stick with them, and let in only the images that support the connection and feel organic. The passage above would collapse if something like a military jeep were to charge through it. If your image is fire, then ash, smoke, coal, ember extend the metaphor. A well-chosen metaphor can be the through-line in your memoir: the powerful image that subtly connects every element of your plot.

Finding Your Way with an Essay

Lee Martin, who writes fiction and essays as well as memoir, says that his memoir *From Our House* began as essays because he wanted to "try out" the material. Essays opened the floodgates. "The material kept coming to me, and I started the narrative arc," he told me.

As a writer, one of the bargains you make with your material is how you will shape it (or how you will give in to the material's own organic shape.) The personal essay is a tried-and-true form for exploring your relationship to your material, and discovering how deeply you can go with it. The word essay itself comes from the French word *essai*, meaning "try" or "attempt." The form was developed in the sixteenth century by the writer Michel de Montaigne, who turned his frank gaze on everything from the workings of his own body to encountering conjoined twins to his occasional exasperation with reading.

Your bargain with your memoir's form and content comes, in part, from recognizing that although you might have intended to write a sweeping epic, you may instead have an elegant or quirky essay on your hands. Your grief memoir might be composed of a linked series of essays. Perhaps a single essay requires a form new to you like the prose poem, or an essay written in segments connected by a recurring theme.

Kathryn Rhett started out as a poet, and continues to write in that form as well as prose. Other than college essays, she says that *Near Breathing* was her first long-form prose writing. She chose memoir as the form for this story of trauma because for her, "there were too many facts and too much to say" to recapture the story adequately as a poem. "Poetry is line and image and exploration, but in this I wanted to figure out what happened. It wasn't going to work as poetry," she explained. As a poet, though, Rhett wanted to preserve in her prose sensory images and the sounds that good sentences make. Here's an example from the memoir.

> When I sleep I dream of manuscripts I'm editing, papers I'm grading, mortgage applications, all white papers with gray type, gray scrawled lettering I can't read. These sheets have a paisley pattern, which makes as much sense as language, pale amoebas swimming on an inky sea. This afternoon I see myself and Cade in the ceiling light fixture, a piece of moon-glass. Our breaths are invisible rivers. I see her long blondish curls against her navy blue dress, her hazel eyes opening and closing. Her lashes, two crescents.

In this paragraph, her sentences have a consistency of sound as well as story as she repeats the word "papers" and the variety of papers accrue. She also uses the sound of the letter "s" throughout the paragraph, in words like "sleep," "scrawled," or "sheets," as well as in "paisley" and "ceiling," ending with that same sound in "lashes" and "crescents." Sensory imagery is here as well, not only in the insistent repetition of the sound that a letter makes when spoken, but in the description of the light, the paisley pattern, her daughter's hair and eye color and the color of her dress.

Just as Nick Flynn suggested reading a particular passage of his aloud to fully experience the way it flows, read your own work aloud, or have someone read it aloud to you so that you can hear the rhythm of the sentences and the way your words sound.

Here, in *Fantasy Freaks and Gaming Geeks,* Ethan Gilsdorf, who has written travel journalism, leaps from traditionally structured paragraphs about travel that delve into the themes and worlds of fantasy into a bullet-point list that's also a footnote on the page. It's also a stand-alone discussion of the characteristics needed to be a LARPer—someone involved in live action role-playing games.

After exploring England, Lake Geneva, and my own past, I had come to appreciate the potency of fantasy. And after playing the bane of my obsession years, D&D, and feeling quite proud of [his avatar, or game character] "Ethora, Arthropod Smiter," I concluded that it was time for my next step, deeper into the dungeon. But was I ready for LARPing—live action role playing?

A few things you need to know about LARPs:

- LARP is a noun (the game itself); it's also a verb ("I LARPed last weekend). Hence, "Am I LARPing?" "You're a good LARPer!" and "I really like a good LARP."
- Each LARP group differs in its philosophy toward rules, costumes, combat, role-playing, participation, and genre.
- LARP settings can be high fantasy, science fiction, Goth, espionage, or cross-genre like steampunk (Victorian era meets [science fiction.])

His inventory of the requirements of the game and its players continues for five more bullet points. Gilsdorf's technique in this example has a lot to do with bargaining. He's striking a balance between the sweeping fantasy world of the subject matter and the meticulous composition of a list, a form he might be more likely to use as a travel writer and journalist.

Research Matters

Just the thought of research makes some writers immediately eager to do absolutely anything else. Research bores them and keeps them from creating, or research seems daunting, with no clear place to start. For other writers, there's the very real possibility of setting off down the path of inquiry and getting lost. You may become so immersed in the hunt itself or the revealing details you find that you run the risk of forgetting why you thought your uncle's letters from the Korean War would be useful to your memoir in the first place. But there's more to writing than sitting at a desk, and there's more to research than the library. In her elegant memoir *One Writer's Beginnings*, Eudora Welty remembers a comment a literary critic made about one of her early short stories. She had written that the moon rose in the west, and learned later that she had been wrong. To me, she captures the simple value of good research in this single sentence: "Always put your moon in the right part of the sky."

When Research Is Time Travel

The adult you, writing your story, intersects with what the younger you remembers. Going on a field trip back to the sidewalks where your younger self played, or turning your kitchen into a time machine and cooking, then tasting, the dessert made the same way that your grandmother made it are the pieces of research that give true authority to writing. There's bargaining here, too: the neighborhood where you grew up may no longer exist, or you may live too far away to visit easily, so you may have to find one that's similar. If the ingredients your *yia yia* used required rosewater and you don't happen to have any on hand, your research will involve a trip to a specialty food store. Once you're there, the scents or the way the packaging looks stir more memories or inspire new questions.

Once you take your first research field trip, you'll find that there's no substitute for visiting an elementary school like yours and hearing again how the tiled hallways echo your footsteps, or how the sunlight looks filtered through the murky glass in the cafeteria windows. You're researching the sensory experience of being in these places, and making active, first-person comparisons between how you as an eight-year-old slid around in chairs that you can barely squeeze into now.

If the younger you in your story is a small child, then your time travel will drop you into places where you are now suddenly taller, where what was once an endless walk from your piano teacher's apartment to the bus stop has become just a few short blocks, and the beauty parlor where your grandmother had her hair rinsed pale blue every week is now an upscale clothing boutique.

The emotion that you feel and the questions you want to ask about how and when things changed are part of the story in writing a grief memoir. If you choose to place your current self in a scene in which you make the effort to retrace your steps or track someone down, these emotions and questions can become elements in a scene. Time-travel research is invaluable for capturing sensory elements that you may have forgotten or have come to distrust with the passage of time or the intrusion of other people's stories.

MY STORY:

For me, time-travel research meant visiting the children's hospital where Susie and Sarah often stayed for weeks at a time. Our family celebrated Susie's eighth birthday—

her last—in that hospital. I have a snapshot of Susie from that day. She's wearing a red sundress patterned like a bandana, and she's posing in the modern sculpture garden on the hospital grounds. She's alone in the shot, facing the camera and leaning against white curved pillars that look to me like teeth. She looks tired. She looks like a girl you'd like to know.

It took a few weeks of thinking about it for me to summon the nerve to visit the hospital. I didn't want to go back. I remembered my young self there as scared, guilty, and sorrowful, but I'd already started writing about the whispering ease of the automatic doors into the lobby, the steam smell of the cafeteria—and I had this old snapshot. I knew that in order for my book to be accurate and for me to feel confident that I had written tough material in the best way I knew how, I had to go. One day I just did it: I stuck my hand into the fire.

I parked in the visitor's lot, walked in the front door— yes, the doors whispered and slid aside much as they had once upon a time. The furniture in the lobby had been updated from the vinyl sixties-era couches, but the floor plan was the same. My muscle memory was automatic. My feet led me to the patient elevators, to the gift shop, and down a hallway to the cafeteria.

I probably should have signed in, but no one asked me to. I must have carried myself like I belonged there. The sculpture garden was what I had come for, and after my self-guided tour of the (mostly) public areas of the hospital, I walked out to what would have been the sculpture garden. But the curved concrete sculpture was no longer there. Instead, the garden had lush landscaping, a wheelchair-friendly path, bird feeders, a teenaged patient on a bench with his family, and a nurse getting some sun. I was sure that when I stepped through those doors I'd be back in 1970, a time traveler where I'd find my smiling little sister posed on her birthday.

I knew better, but I still went in search of that moment.

What I got from my research was reassurance that the way I remembered the hospital smelling is exactly how it still smelled (disinfectant, steam, cafeteria food, perfume, the plasticky tang of antibiotics). My memories about how the place was laid out were proven accurate: yes, you took a right from the front doors to get to the patient elevators. The receptionist's station had been modernized, but was still in the corner.

I asked a security guard about the sculpture garden. It had been there, he said (and I had the photo to prove it, if only to myself) but a few years before, the trustees decided to change it. It's a lovely garden now, too.

Heart thumping, I survived to write another day. And the bargain I made with myself? If I didn't go back to that hospital where my sisters, parents, and I had been so afraid and so reliant on each other, the place would always loom larger than life in my memory, my imagination, and my heart. Those mixed emotions were a part of my story. Even though I knew my sisters were no longer in beds upstairs and our father was no longer grinding his cigarettes out in front of the sliding door, I had to see it in present day to show these facts to my writer-self and my everyday-self. The panic and sorrow that swirled in me as I visited that familiar place belonged on the page now, no longer in my throat.

So what would have happened if my sensory memory and my facts were proven wrong in my research? How would I have written those scenes if that photo of Susie lounging among the sculptures had been taken not at the hospital, but at some anonymous park?

I would still have a story. That story would be about the bargaining I would do and why I believed what I did until my research proved otherwise. Those sections in my memoir would have been about why I had believed the hospital garden to be the setting for my photograph, and how my research led me to different information. I could have written about learning that I'd been wrong and that the photo of Susie was from a happier time than a hospital stay, and that I had come to see all photos of my sister under the shadow of a hospital.

Writing a memoir helps you see your life differently: negotiating your understanding of your loss and grief with two versions of yourself, the you before your loss, and after. "Disagreeing with your earlier self is the life-blood of memoir," Ethan Gilsdorf points out. One of the reasons that readers turn to memoir is to watch the writer reevaluate his past and engage in a kind of conversation between his past and present selves. "Writers shouldn't keep those revelations and changing ideas of the self from the reader," he adds. I agree, and when I read a good memoir, the story of the writer's coming to an understanding of herself engages me as much as, and sometimes more, than the nominal chain of events. For example, in Alexandra Fuller's memoir, *Don't Let's Go to the Dogs Tonight: An African Childhood*, she writes about growing up in Rhodesia (now Zimbabwe) during the 1970s, when the country experienced a civil war. One of the forces that draws me to her memoir is the way she writes about her parents' racism and her unwillingness to think as they do.

Practical Experts

Another approach to research is to tag along with an expert. If you're writing about wildlife and land conservation, find out if attending the local meetings of an advocacy group or taking a guided walk with the sea-turtle rescue team or a raptor reha-bilitation organization would give you the kind of first-person, up-close information you need. If you're writing about crime or urban blight, many communities offer "ride-alongs" with their police force. If there's a weapon in your memoir, there may be a shooting range near you where you can take a lesson and feel the burden of a pistol in your hand. An entertainment industry scene in your memoir? Check with your local tourism board; they'll know if a movie's filming in town and how to apply to be an extra.

If you're not employed in the medical profession, it's unlikely that you would be able to observe a live surgical procedure to get a sense of what happened to a loved one during their operation. However, some pretty fascinating video recordings of surgery, with explanatory narration, are available on the Internet.

Author Ian Frazier wrote about the appeal of research in his essay "Looking for My Family," which appears in the anthology *Inventing the Truth*. After his father's Alzheimer's disease and death and his mother's subsequent death, Frazier and his siblings sorted through their parents' belongings. Frazier, a magazine journalist, humorist, and, at the time, the author of one nonfiction book, *Great Plains* (he has written many more since then) sorted through his parents' letters, his mother's purses, his father's ties, and more, examining them and organizing them into boxes he called "the mom museum" and "the dad museum." He asks himself about the stories those objects can provide for him. This research—his museums—gave deeper meaning to his parents' lives in his book *Family*, which chronicles his examination of his own family's history as far back as the Revolutionary War.

When I read his essay—and I teach it often—I feel as if he's talking directly to me about my own love for research. When I hold something like a piece of jewelry or a postcard that belonged to someone I cared about, the object sometimes matters more to me than it may have mattered to them. It becomes more than an artifact: it's a portal into the world I'm trying to capture on paper.

The Double-Entry Technique

The double-entry, or dialectical, notebook technique comes from science, but it's perfect for the grief memoirist searching for the stories in her own examination of artifacts. Educators use double-entry notebooks to help students catalogue their personal reactions to other texts. Science students and calculus students use them to test theories, comparing on the bisected page what they think will happen in an experiment with what actually happens.

Some dialectical notebooks are premade composition-style notebooks with a horizontal line running across the center of the page. There's graph-paper style above the line and composition-ruled below the line. You can create your own by drawing a line horizontally or vertically, whichever appeals to you, along the middle of the pages in your journal. For the memoir writer, double-entry notebooks help you find the place where writer and research meet, helping you see the connections that will help you create narrative. Your emotions often run high as you excavate the elements that you will use in your grief memoir. A double-entry notebook is a particularly good tool for staying focused and for recognizing the story value of the interaction that you're having with your research. Detailing your research alongside your thoughts and feelings in a double-entry note-book lets you capture your actions and reactions in the same place.

For example, I filled two double-entry notebooks with my research for *Invisible Sisters*. Because I knew I would turn often to thirty years' worth of my own journals, I was a little apprehensive about finding what I needed in the small mountain of personal research ahead of me. In my journals I wanted to find the juxtaposition between the grown woman reading them—me—and the child, teenager, and young woman who had written them—also me. With a double-entry notebook, a pen, and some paper clips (so I could mark the original journal pages if I wanted to go back to them) I read my own old words. When I came to a journal entry that seized my heart or my memory, I picked up the double-entry notebook. Above the line, I wrote the date of the entry that had made me catch my breath, wrote which journal it was in, and what it looked like, and I copied down my own words. Below the line I wrote what I felt while reading that old entry, what else it made me remember, and if I was crying, laughing, or even irritated. Sometimes I merely splotched the page with tears, or wrote how thrilled I was to come across a memory I'd lost.

MY STORY:

Telling my own story of grief also meant doing some digging in medical records. I first envisioned basing the memoir on a comparison of my childhood with my sisters' childhoods. We were three girls from the same home, same parents, with lives so similar and yet so fundamentally different. By the time I was nine, I had begun introducing myself to doctors and lab technicians as "the well sibling." My sisters sometimes spent long stretches of time in hospitals. I visited them, but left at night with one or both parents to go home for dinner, to do homework, and sleep in my own bed. Susie or Sarah stayed behind in a world they came to know well but I could only imagine. So when I really began to write, I set a mandate for myself. I needed to read their hospital records, and look at their lives from a distance to contrast the close lens I already had. Hospital records were a different kind of intimacy than personal journals. They examined the territories of my sisters' bodies, not their emotional lives.

The Health Insurance Portability and Accountability Act of 1996, or HIPAA, protects the privacy of hospital records. I contacted several of the hospitals who had most often cared for my sisters, including Memorial Sloan-

Kettering in New York and Scottish Rite Children's Hospital in Atlanta (then called the Henrietta Egleston Hospital for Children). I explained my quest, and asked to be connected with the communications or public relations office. In every case, the person in the communications office was generous, understanding, and helpful. For reasons related to the privacy law, the records I was requesting (some of which were old enough by then to be in off-site storage) couldn't be released to me without the written approval of the patient's parent or guardian, even though the patients in question were deceased. Their parent was also my parent, and supportive of the project. The hospitals faxed permission forms, my mother and I completed them and faxed them back, and photocopies of the paperwork I requested were sent to me.

Sitting at my desk with three or four folders several inches thick containing duplicates of almost twenty years' worth of my sisters' medical records, I faced the pretty big risk of losing my hold on my story as I examined the minutiae of their illnesses. (And wasn't this memoir about how some of my own childhood disappeared that very same way?) I wanted very much to read these accounts of their days that I hadn't shared, and I knew that I would need to use the medical language that I knew so well—the "accidental expertise" that is still part of who I am. But I didn't want to lose my focus on the effect that the information on those pages would have on me as an adult. That was a big part of the grief I was writing about.

This was my perfect opportunity to use a double-entry notebook. As I read and reacted to the pages, I described as objectively as I could the material I was reading. I wrote the date and source hospital, the doctor's comments that had caught my attention, and other factual items such as length of a surgery, Susie or Sarah's height or weight, or the dosage for a medication. On the bottom half of the page, I let my emotions and senses loose. I wrote how the photocopies felt in my hand. I wrote if a name on a page triggered a memory, no matter if it was immediately relevant or not. I noted if I began to cry, got angry, or wanted to push the stack away from me and retreat entirely from this unnerving view of my sisters through strangers' eyes. I wrote about the awkward pride I still had in my sorely gotten skill of reading medical jargon.

With double-entry notebooks, and my colored pens, paper clips, sticky notes, and a paperback medical dictionary, I read about the days in my sisters' lives that up until then I could only imagine. I saw the sisters I mourned and missed every day through the eyes of their physicians, nurses, and lab technicians. And through them, I saw myself. In the memoir, I wrote about the experience this way:

> Scouring files filled with details of their days that I had never known, I wept for my sisters for what felt like the first time. There is Sarah, eight years old, afraid of a bone marrow biopsy, carried from the exam room "in father's arms." There is Susie, hallucinating for reasons that the attending physician recorded as "somewhat confusing." Maybe her delirium was a side effect of her steroids, her antinausea medication, or her painkillers. Maybe, he noted, her mental state was the result of her "disease process."

If I go backward in the research process, I turn to these specific notes from a surgical record for Sarah dated December 13, 1979, for a "left myringotomy" or an incision in her left eardrum for "serious otitis media," an ear infection.

> The patient was draped and prepped with Betadine. An operating microscope with 6 magnification was introduced into the field and the left eardrum was visualized.

That report continues for two detailed paragraphs, with language like "anterior-inferior quadrant," "Teflon drainage tube," and "aspirated."

The blank space at the top right of the document labeled KIND OF ANESTHESIA is filled in with the typewritten words "Sodium pentothal," "nitrous oxide," "oxygen," "oroendotracheal intubation."

The typeface is Arial, the page is a photocopy, and the original had punch-holes on top for her chart. It's one sheet in an inch-thick cluster of pages that I held together with a black clip, part of a larger stack held together with more clips.

And my introspective comments on these facts for the other side of the notebook's line? I'll excerpt them here.

What was it like then to live this, they can't get out from under it.

Facts about Sarah I didn't know. She was allergic to Bactrim . . . what are the life things, human things I didn't know?

Age 14, busted eardrum and mastoiditis from infection. I am such a pussy compared . . .

Because this was my journal, I wrote in short, sometimes grammatically incorrect sentences. Other times I drew, or scrawled words and shapes because I was angry, confused, or high—my way of escaping my surroundings, but not my journals.

The contrasts between Sarah's surgical record and my double-entry notebook assessments don't make an entire book, or even an entire scene. They're just part of the bargaining that takes place when you work to find out where the story lies: in "the life things . . . I didn't know."

> TIP: If you are requesting medical records for your own
> research, ask a representative from the hospital or medical
> center about their procedures for doing so. Ask to be
> connected to the public information department or
> communications office. Follow the law, but don't be afraid
> to ask respectfully for what you want. If you're unable to get
> access to the outside sources that you feel you need, remember
> that the absence or denial of those records can contribute to
> your memoir, too. Try writing about why you wanted them,
> why you couldn't get them, and what you still don't know as
> a result.

You the Reporter

Approaching your story with the same skills that a reporter would use brings depth and perspective that serves
memoir well. Blending journalism with memoir integrates the
factual with the personal. You expand your writing into something that "hard news" doesn't permit—uncovering the story
around you as you participate as a character in the story itself.
For example, author Sandra Beasley mixes reporting with personal experience in her memoir *Don't Kill the Birthday Girl: Tales
from an Allergic Life*. When we talked about why she chose to
write this way, she told me, "the subject of food allergies is on
one hand an objective, medicalized subject, but on the other
hand is incredibly subjective in terms of individual reactions
and experience." In her memoir, she writes about her severe,
and in some cases, life-threatening allergies to a variety of sub-
stances, including dairy products, cucumber, dust, and wool.
"The generational response to how to treat severe allergies, and
what responsibility society has to protect allergic kids, is so different today versus ten or twenty years ago," she says. "I was
drawn to research because I wanted to create a vocabulary of
fact to allow us to communicate."

In this example from *Don't Kill the Birthday Girl*, she writes of an allergy attack, framing her personal experience within a scientific explanation, striking a balance—a bargain—between research and memoir.

> A reaction can start within seconds, or accumulate over a period of several hours. Some scientists believe delayed reactions result from a different antibody response— immunoglobulin G, or IgG—particularly primed to respond to such allergens as milk, wheat, and corn. After one ill-fated dinner party, I was awakened in the middle of the night by an attack I thought I'd tamed before going to bed, with a reaction much worse than the one I'd had earlier. That's considered a biphasic reaction.

Her modulated, factual presentation in this passage doesn't lessen the information about the danger of a serious allergy attack, but puts it in a context beyond her own: a young woman whose ingestion of a salad that touched another diner's cheese resulted in a late-night ambulance call.

Being a reporter in your own life lets you "dig into the provenance of life, and opens your eyes to storytelling possibilities," says Hank Klibanoff, coauthor of the Pulitzer Prize–winning *The Race Beat: The Press, the Civil Rights Struggle, and the Awakening of a Nation*. Klibanoff, a veteran reporter and editor, and the James M. Cox Jr. Professor of Journalism at Emory University, believes that a memoirist must be passionate about her story. Apply that passion to exploration, he suggests. If you're searching for "the house that you think used to be there, and you see an old person in a wheelchair, go see if that person has a memory that can help you."

Another way to be a reporter is by using microfilm records in libraries. Microfilm records are a time machine, he says, that lets you see much more than you're looking for. For example, if you're searching newspaper records for coverage of your mother's childhood town during a wildfire, you might find a story on that same page about a pet parade in a neighboring town. You may not think at first that you want this information, but you have in front of you an image of the culture of the community, and you start to wonder what your parents and their friends, as kids, did with their spare time. One ad in the paper will tell you what their parents paid for school clothes, another what they might have watched on television.

Applying reporting techniques to the questions you have about your own life can broaden your narrative and your perspective, putting your story in the larger framework of the world in which it took place. Your memoir of grief becomes more universal this way, too. A reader may find similarities to themselves in your story, and say, as they have to me, "my father was active in the Southern labor movement, too."

Robin Hemley found that in writing his memoir *Nola: A Memoir of Faith, Art, and Madness,* he became a detective on the trail of the story of his sister Nola's mental illness and death and his mother's life before he was born. He writes in the beginning of that memoir that,

> Uncovering the facts, not even the facts but the feelings of my sister's and mother's lives, has become a detective story for me.

"The first detective act is to try to peer through the keyhole into who you really are," he explains. Hemley recommends that authors of longer memoir do a kind of detective work about the focus of their book, asking themselves what their book is about, then asking themselves that same question again, and finally, asking themselves once again what it's *really* about. Digging deeply this way, you've started your detective work, he explains.

Just a few of the "detective" elements Hemley uses in this memoir are his parents' divorce documents, and the transcript of a session he had with a hypnotist. These are just some of the clues that he uses to uncover the story as a whole.

For Neil White, thinking like a particular reporter he idolized helped him get through his days in prison. "It dawned on me, wearing a prison uniform and mopping the floor, that even George Plimpton couldn't weasel his way into a leprosarium," he told me.

When he was in his twenties, White launched an alternative newspaper in Oxford, Mississippi. Willie Morris, the acclaimed author and editor of *Harper's* magazine was then writer-in-residence at The University of Mississippi. White was lucky—Morris introduced him to his idol, reporter George Plimpton.

> I'd always dreamed of being an undercover journalist, secretly documenting conspiratorial practices and exploring hidden worlds. . . . I wanted to know everything he knew about immersion into a strange culture, clandestine reporting, and impersonation. I wanted to know what it felt like to go undercover, to write about things no one has any business knowing . . .
>
> Now, as I mopped the [prison] cafeteria floor, a hundred checkered blocks at a time, I imagined what Plimpton would do in my place. And it was obvious. He would write about it.

Writing about his experience in prison and imagining the award he would someday receive for his writing became White's *modus operandi* while he lived through the grief he felt in prison. He reported to himself on his daily life in order to make it through that daily life.

When you include other people's perspectives, like the weather or fashions on a certain date or even what it cost to gas up a Chevy, you lift some of the responsibility from your flawed, human memory. Your plot moves forward, pushed by friction created as you write about how you remember one thing but the facts insist on another, or as you marvel at the way facts and memory connect in a smooth parallel.

Lee Martin says about the research he conducted for his memoir, *From Our House*, that "as a writer, I needed to honor the facts of my father's life." He believes that research immerses you in the particulars of the people in the world you're retrieving. In the passage below, Martin didn't want to simply describe the survey map of the family farm, but imbue the reader with a sense of what he and his parents were about to lose, a world "safe and knowable" as they move to the city.

This section puts the reader in motion across this particular piece of land, using sensory details like the smell of the thawing earth and the sound of the tractor at work. Once this physical presence is established, Martin begins to describe the land in the official language of a surveyor, a tone divested of the emotion he and his forebears attached to their home.

> I knew the smell of the earth thawing, the sounds of peepers trilling in the night at our pond, the taste of a blade of grass, the cool air at dusk, the rumble of my father's tractor, the spark of its headlights back and forth across the field. I knew the lay of our eighty acres: the long field that stretched back to the tree line, the creek we had to cross to reach the back forty. . . . My great-grandfather had acquired the land in 1884, had given it over to my grandfather in 1919, who had then deeded it to my father in 1940, one year before my grandfather's death. Our part of southeastern Illinois had been surveyed and divided neatly into sections. We owned, according to the language of the deed, "The South Half (S ½) of the Northwest Quarter (NW ¼) of Section 18, Township 2 North, Range 13 West, of the Second P.M. (Prime Meridian), containing eighty (80) acres, more or less." To me, it was

nearly the world, and I didn't know, that spring and summer of 1963, that I was about to leave it.

The emotion in the beginning of the section surfaces again in the last sentence, where the exteriority of detailed research combines with the interiority of memoir, and the reader feels deeply for the boy who, that summer, didn't know he would have to look back.

Libraries as Resources

When I was writing my memoir, I spent several afternoons curled up in a comfortable oversized chair in Emory University's main library, taking notes from a huge medical textbook called *Harrison's Principles of Internal Medicine*. I didn't know the name of any medical textbook when I started my memoir, so I asked a research librarian. They know everything. I could look up the current definitions, treatments, and etiology for the illnesses that took my sisters' lives on any number of reliable medical sites online. But it wasn't so easy to find out what a physician in 1968 would have on hand about Acute Lymphocytic Leukemia and Kostmann's syndrome to help him determine what was happening to them and how to treat it.

I had other questions that required a different library. The Georgia State University library has a special collection of materials related to the local history of the Southern labor movement. Using a special collection sometimes requires an appointment, so I made one and explained the very little I knew about what I was looking for. My father had mentioned casually that he'd heard that the records from the labor union where he had worked had gone to that library. He was curious about them, and I was, too. He was dying, and his home was then more than a thousand miles from Georgia. I decided to look up the records for him, and for myself, too.

When I came in on my appointed day and hour, the librarian had arranged half a dozen cardboard boxes on a long table. Wearing the white gloves she had given me to prevent the oils on my skin from damaging the aging paper, I extracted a desk diary that I remembered lying open across my parents' bed. I held file folders of my father's office correspondence, more neatly organized than they had ever been when they covered his law office desk. I read memos that would have meant nothing to me as a child, but told me as an adult that he had abandoned a company car in a fit of pique. I read memos about cases that he had talked about at the dinner table, the names of mills and towns coming back to me like a film montage. I looked at phone messages on square pink note-slips initialed by secretaries who suddenly reappeared in my mind, tall, kind, and impossibly poised.

I made a list of the holdings for my father so he would have a sense of how his past contributed to the library. And when I wrote my memoir, I went back with a double-entry notebook and got to work.

TIP: Libraries are reservoirs of specialized knowledge. A historical society library may have records of deed and property ownership, period telephone books, even menus from society banquets and cultural events. If you can't remember the name of the street your best friend lived on in high school and you really need to know it, a historical society library will have the city directory for that year. Do some time travel and use that directory. A library that specializes in technology, such as a college or company library, may have patents, scientific research, and correspondence between leaders in the field.

The world opens up to a writer using an archive. At Georgia State University, Morna Gerrard, who is the Women's Collection Archivist in the Special Collections, told me when I visited her that people love the visual and tangible results they get from researching in archives. She collects oral histories for the archive, and told me that hearing the voices and seeing video of individuals talking about their experiences "lights a fire" in people who come to see and hear them. "It's amazing to hear someone's voice. It's human and emotional, you can see them laughing or sad," she said. This kind of research can be emotional for the archivist as well as the researcher. She has wept with her subjects while recording digital interviews about domestic violence. "By talking about it and knowing that you're part of this body of other histories, it's almost like a club: you've shared yourself," she says.

She began her career at the National Archives of Scotland. She has catalogued artifacts as diverse as a letter written by Mary, Queen of Scots to her mother in the sixteenth century to a gas mask from the bombing of a feminist women's health center in the nineteen eighties. She told me that artifacts like these, and oral histories, newsletters, hand-drawn maps, recipes, T-shirts, and a wealth of similar items are what make archival research a one-of-a-kind journey into the history of an individual and moments in their daily lives.

There are ethical considerations to bear in mind when using material from an archive. The first is to acknowledge the archive in your book. It's good manners, and there may be legal requirements as well. Like a character in a fairy tale, you're leaving a trail of bread crumbs for other authors and researchers who might read your work and find that they have similar interests. You've led them to a useful source.

Gerrard told me that writers might be surprised at what they have at their fingertips. "If your parents had businesses they may have kept records. There may be a recipe book or journals," she says. Describing her reading of her own grandmother's recipes from World War II, Gerard says, "there was rationing, so what do the ingredients tell you?" For example, if sugar was rationed, but there's a recipe for a cake, what did the cook use to make do? If they saved coupons and splurged on sugar, what was the special occasion?

Consider the generations who will come after you, too.

Make sure to identify people, places, and dates on the backs of photographs that are a part of your life now. Your memoir will become a living piece of an informal cultural archive.

Archives are easy to find. Universities often have them. So do city and state historical societies, even businesses and organizations. Gerrard suggests doing an Internet search combining your topic with your location, plus the word "archives," to get started.

Using an archive is a different experience than using a library. For one thing, they aren't usually collections of shelved books that you can take down and read at will. "There are thousands of boxes of files to look through, and you may not find what you intend to find," Gerrard says. "There's a lot of serendipity when you're visiting the folders." Plan on staying for at least a few hours.

I love her choice of the word "visiting." That sums up my love for the homey feeling that archives can provide; I'm visiting with people's artifacts that are the tangible evidence of their ideas and daily lives. "Visit" is so much more of an intimate, approachable word than "research" or "investigation."

When Artifacts Are Too Hot to Handle

I have no photograph of her that is any good, C. S. Lewis wrote of his wife in *A Grief Observed*.

> I cannot even see her face distinctly in my imagination. . . . We have seen the faces of those we know best so variously, from so many angles, in so many lights, with so many expressions—waking, sleeping, laughing, crying, eating, talking, thinking—that all the impressions crowd into our memory together and cancel out into a mere blur. But her voice is still vivid. The remembered voice—that can turn me at any moment into a whimpering child.

Some of what we remember as we write through grief comes and goes, flickering under our grasp like a flame turned to vapor. Other things we can't forget, no matter how hard we try to push an image or sound from our minds. I can remember my sister Sarah's quiet voice, and the tense sound of our father's voice, but I can no longer remember the sound of my sister Susie's voice, and all these years later, my grief is still too strong to listen to the only tape recording of her voice that I own.

Writing through your grief, you know before you begin that parts of your story will turn you, for a time, into that "whimpering child." There may be pieces of your story that you grieve so strongly you have to leave them alone, maybe for the moment, maybe for longer.

There are some artifacts from my story that I could have turned to when I wrote my memoir, but I chose not to revisit them because I knew that then, and maybe forever, the sadness they'll provoke outweighs the reward for me. I have a reel-to-reel tape recording from the early nineteen sixties of Susie and me playing. We're both too young for school. Something we said or the sounds of our play must have inspired an adult to capture those moments. I have an answering machine tape with what I know is an ordinary message from Sarah from a few weeks before she died. A videotape of my father's last birthday party, a box of photographs from a trip to London my mother, my husband, and I took a decade ago, all occupy that space I could label "artifacts from a family that has dwindled." I keep all these things because even though they're too emotionally hot for me to look at or listen to, I still need to know that these moments and the people who inhabited them are loved. I know that I may never be ready to be catapulted back to listening to Susie and me playing before our lives turned around forever.

Imagine that writers crafting the true stories of their grief are like snails, leaving nearly invisible trails behind as they traverse their lives. If you return to a place where you lived years ago, will you catch a glimpse of your former self ducking behind the door or obscured by the sun's glare in a window? Even though I know better, sometimes I feel that if I look hard enough, I can.

Photographs can be handled, audio tapes can be popped into a cassette player or threaded onto a reel to reel, video cassettes can be transferred to disc and watched. Physical artifacts generate sensory memory the same way that a field trip can, creating a kind of 360-degree experience for you as you write about your loss and subsequent experience.

Author Robin Hemley cautions against the overuse of photographs as illustrations in a memoir. He compares them to visual exclamation marks, an effort to prop up what might be a lackluster sentence without the accompanying image. Using photographs as writing prompts and in research, however, has what he calls a kind of "magic property." When we talked, he explained that photographs have the power to bring an author back to what he describes as a "particular scissored-out moment" in time, allowing the writer's imagination to reach beyond what the photograph depicts. You might look at a photograph of the façade of your childhood home, and even though the image doesn't show the tree root you always tripped over by the front steps, or the sound of the washing machine churning in the laundry room just down the hall, you can mentally fill in what you know was there, just past the edges of the picture.

Even a stranger's photo can evoke images and memories that are purely our own. I bought a photograph at a flea market showing a frozen moment in a children's pageant from sometime before nineteen twenty, estimating by the appearance of the adults' clothing. Every child in the picture wears a costume for a part in a play of *Alice's Adventures in Wonderland*: a March Hare mask, a few chest-sized playing cards (long before the film *The Manchurian Candidate*), a Mad Hatter, and several dormice. Each child pulls a serious face—even the masks look serious—except for one little girl in the front row. She's delighted to be there, and her grin engages me from across time. She must be a very old woman now if she's still living, but she's relevant to my writing about grief for the best of reasons: who-ever she is, she's the embodiment of that genuine little-kid ex-citement that I saw in my sisters and felt in myself when we were small. And she reminds me of another photo of someone I did know: my mother's mother at about the age of five, in a frilly dress and a lovable smile, dwarfed by the flowered head-dress she's wearing in a pageant in Dorchester, Massachusetts, in about 1905. What's just beyond the photo's edges can tap a deep vein for a memoirist, even if that photo is torn or faded or shows a face we can't name.

MY STORY:

About a year after my father died, my husband and I took a trip to Memphis, Tennessee. We wanted to see Grace-land for the kitsch and a nostalgic thrill for the pioneering younger Elvis, who was long gone by the time we picked up the rock-and-roll habit. As our vacation weekend came to a close, we found ourselves at a diner near the National Civil Rights Museum, which is housed in what had been the Lorraine Motel, where Dr. Martin Luther King was assassinated in 1968. My husband wanted to go to the museum. I hesitated, not because I lacked admiration for what the museum represented, but because I was positive that there couldn't be anything there that I hadn't learned at my father's knee, and sometimes witnessed firsthand. But I knew that I would be unhappy with myself if I left Memphis without paying my respects. We finished our breakfast and crossed the street to the low-slung 1950s brick building.

I remember now that the museum was excellent, but what's indelible in my memory is a photograph I came face-to-face with at the end of an exhibit leading to the exit. The photograph was a black-and-white shot of my father, sitting on a curb in Memphis four days after

Dr. King was killed. My father is holding a white placard reading HONOR KING: END RACISM. Beside him is another man holding a placard reading UNION JUSTICE NOW. Both men wear dark suits and skinny ties. They look exhausted. They are also heartbroken: their expressions as they look directly into the camera are unmistakable. My father a white man, his friend black—a man I recall from my childhood, but whose name I can't remember no matter how hard I try.

The caption on the picture didn't name them. It only called the two men "unidentified." To the photographer, these were just two people emblematic of many in a terrible time. But to me, this was not an unidentified man. This was my father.

I processed all of this information in seconds. Someone watching would have seen a woman approaching a photograph, stopping in her tracks, gasping once, and bursting into tears. My father had died less than a year earlier, and here was his face on a museum wall. He hadn't known about the photo, I was sure. He would have been proud of it. He would have told me about it, and certainly more than once.

In the picture my father was young, the very beginning of the losses that would shape his life appearing in the way he sprawled on the curb and in the lost look in his eyes. Susie and Sarah were both newly sick then, Susie not yet six, Sarah still a toddler. His life was changing quickly, and on that day, a stranger had frozen my father in time. His two youngest daughters were dying and his hero had been murdered. In that picture I saw what might have been the moment of my father's change from idealist to cynic.

I felt an ironic and accidental personal injustice in a site dedicated to justice. One person who could identify him best—me—had nearly chosen not to come to the museum. Shaken, I asked a museum guard to take me to an administrator. He did, and I explained to her what had just happened and how important it was that the names of the people in the picture be known. She gave me the contact information for the photographer whose work was being showcased in that exhibit, a man named Benedict Fernandez. The photos were from his book called *Countdown to Eternity*.

I corresponded with him and felt a circle closing. I wish that I could also remember my father's friend's name, if I ever knew it to begin with. I hope that someone in his family has seen the photograph, or that he has, if he's still living.

A visitor to that exhibit or a reader perusing the photo book it was based on sees a documentary photograph of two weary men on a day that changed countless people. I see my father, and the haze of sorrow that surrounded him. I can hear the lyrics to the protest songs that I learned along with my counting songs and alphabet songs. I smell his cigarettes: the four packs of Pall Mall unfiltered that he smoked every day for years. I cringe from the terse bark of his voice in anger, and the elegant, rolling pace when he recited poems. I see a picture and get a story that only I can write.

In *From Our House*, Lee Martin writes of a snapshot he took as a teenager of his family's new home.

> When I look at the photograph now, I see the creases at the corners where my father clamped it between the prongs of his hook as he took it from his shirt pocket to show to people.

A person unfamiliar with the family and their story might see merely a slightly damaged old snapshot. The author sees the reason for the damage to the photograph's corners, and it's from there, more than the image in the photo itself, that Martin creates his narrative of loss.

Broken things have value for the grief memoirist in their very brokenness. We're no longer pristine or in our unbroken state, and damaged items are often more evocative of story than material objects unscarred. Can you imagine the Liberty Bell without its storied crack?

The technology of images is changing as digital media rapidly replaces analogue. As I write, I wonder what will constitute an artifact for someone else. A writer in the near future may have fewer sensory elements to generate memories, without the Polaroid snapshot we turn sideways to read the fading date printed on the margin, the delicate edges of a vinyl LP we balance with our fingertips, or the musty scent of an old book under our noses. For example, you may be reading this on a screen rather than on paper, or listening to music via a digital file instead of a CD. And for some writers, that progress is also a kind of loss.

Their Own Words

Perhaps you've received more education than a relative, or your travels through life have created a different perspective on culture, religion, or politics than the people you grew up with. This might mean that the author of a letter you want to include in your memoir used poor grammar or spelling, or their worldview was different from yours. Including their words and opinions in your memoir is another way that you bargain with your story. While the story is of your grief told from your perspective, your life has been shaped in some way by the authors of these artifacts. Including them in their natural voice is part of the ongoing work of broadening your story and connecting it to place and time. They are elements of memoir for the author trying understand how she has changed.

Keeping the inaccurate spellings or the off-putting opinions presents that character as they truly are or were, and gives the reader—and you, as the author—a point of conflict or opposition in your story of loss. You are not like them. Or you were like them, and are no longer. Or you didn't think you were like them, but you learn that you are. That's conflict, and with it, your story moves forward.

Janisse Ray chose to reproduce her seventy-five-year-old grandfather's nonstandard spelling in his letters to her, letters full of love, with "ancer" for answer, and "squarles" for squirrels. Ray points out that the person writing the letter is an "interesting character in [his] own right." As an author, she could have written an expository statement that tells us he attended school until seventh grade, but we know this more profoundly when we read portions of his letters in their original voice. This is "show, don't tell," in action. This is also love and respect.

The Ethics of Memoir

Writing a memoir means that your true story includes other people. In a memoir about grief, even if you suffer that grief alone, other people were involved in the story at some point.

Memoir writers have a certain responsibility to the other people in their stories. You may need their permission to be included or to use their real names. You may feel strongly that people should know they're mentioned by name in the book. Private files like medical records or legal documents may need to be officially released to you by the hospital or agency that retains them.

You already know the first rule of memoir: don't lie. Here's where you do a gut check and decide if you're genuinely comfortable telling your truth in print, knowing that other people—strangers as well as loved ones—might read it. If you're not, turn your talent to fiction.

Writing a memoir requires ethical judgment calls. You may wonder how to determine if it's okay to use real names or places in the book, or how to make sure that you have the correct permission you need to use legal documents, family letters and photos, or medical records. Maybe you've never thought about it at all, and here I am giving you something else to think about.

Unlike journalists, authors of memoir are free to change names, particularly if they indicate they've done so in a disclaimer like the example earlier in this book. But like journalism, identifying a character with a moniker like "anonymous" can undermine your credibility as an author.

If you can, ask permission of the people you mention by name. You may want to change the names of people you can't get in touch with. As a general rule, public figures and the deceased can't be libeled under United States law. In my memoir, I used the real names of everyone in my family, of two public figures—one dead, one living—and several of my closest friends, whose permission I had obtained by email. Another friend didn't want me to use her name simply because she's not comfortable in the public eye, so I changed it. I had lost touch with several other friends who appeared in the book, and out of respect for their privacy, changed their names.

Natasha Trethewey says she agonized about how to tell her brother's story within *Beyond Katrina*. She worried "about the reader who would say 'oh this guy is just some drug dealer' and not be able to connect with him and the devastation of his life." She worried most, she says, about describing him in the courtroom, his shoulders hunched. "Who would want to see himself presented like that, not looking strong and heroic?" she told me. She kept her brother informed about what she was writing, and let him read the work. "I know he feels it was a sympathetic portrayal of him," she says, adding that he's attended several readings, and has seen that audiences don't view him as "one of society's throwaways."

Hank Klibanoff believes that while journalism—his beat—

and memoir don't always operate under the same ethical guide-lines, he offers four approaches from the newsroom that an author can use to assess her ethical approach to her memoir. These are adapted from the textbook *The Ethical Journalist: Making Responsible Decisions in the Pursuit of News*, by Gene Fore-man, which Klibanoff uses in his classroom. The first is "rule-based thinking," which is the author's duty to do the right thing regardless of the outcome. The second, "ends-based thinking," means that the author weighs the value of the work to herself and the community against the potential consequences, which she may not always foresee. The third, which is the one under which I try to operate, is the Golden Rule, or "do unto others as you would have them do unto you." The last is the Golden Mean, in which the writer finds his or her own middle ground.

So, how does the Golden Rule apply to grief memoir? *Don't* write for revenge. *Do* put yourself in the other person's shoes. Tell your emotional truth.

Emotional truth isn't always provable truth. Emotional truth is when you know that you had a crush on that girl next door when you were both in kindergarten, a love that made you giddy, was filled with sunshine and mown grass and skinned knees, but you can not for the life of you remember her name. It might have been Rachel, Robin, or Rosie, but the sense of that love sent you on a quest until you met the woman you married, someone more perfect than your kindergarten love. The emo-tional truth in this scenario is the power of that first crush, not the long-ago girl's correct name.

You could go on a tremendous search through social net-working sites and shoeboxes of photographs, trying to jog your memory of her name, or you could choose to write using a signal phrase such as "I think," or "I believe," or even, "I don't remem-ber." The emotional truth is that your feelings in that friendship molded you and set your course. But because memoirists are not journalists, we allow our stories to be subjective, originating from our own memories, which we know have gaps and ques-tions as well as clear moments of both great pain and joy.

Unlike emotional truth, provable truth are facts that can be proven, and if misrepresented, are a detriment to your integrity as an author. Provable truth is something you and others can verify, that is as true to you as it is to someone else. For example, when I was ten, not long after Susie died, my family took a vacation to Jamaica. When I tell this story now, people sigh with delight imagining a family healing in a blue-water Caribbean paradise. In those days, Jamaica wasn't the tourist destination it is now, and even if it had been, none of us were ready for fun. As I wrote about my family's trip, I kept seeing myself as a child, gagging and refusing to eat ackee at our Jamaican breakfast table. My sensory memories came back full force. The breakfast tasted to me like burned motor oil and smelled like talcum power. This was emotionally true, but I knew it couldn't be factual.

As I wrote, I wondered why I had hated the taste of ackee so vehemently. Was it really as bad as I remembered? I had vague memories of someone picking it from a tree, but I wasn't certain if that was accurate. I didn't know if it was a fruit or a vegetable.

The provable truth was easy to find in an encyclopedia or online. Ackee is a fruit, it does grow on trees, and is, in fact, a national fruit of Jamaica. The pictures I saw showed the same fat-seeded yellow flesh that I saw in my mind's eye. This made me confident that I had the basic facts right.

But my reactions to the fruit's taste were emotional memory. I asked a few students from Caribbean families how they liked ackee. They liked it very much. I was in an understandably negative frame of mind the summer I was ten, but now I wasn't comfortable writing about the bad taste that I remembered so well. I wanted to make sure that the ten-year-old me and the adult me were in agreement, or find a difference that I could write about. So I printed a recipe from the Internet, went to an international market, bought canned ackee (there was none fresh where I live) and cooked a facsimile of that breakfast. I ate it. And then I knew that my memories were made of equal parts provable truth and emotional truth. Ackee is a fruit that grows on a tree. Some people like the taste, but it still didn't appeal to me.

TIP: Journalism is objective, seeking truth from all sides. The Society of Professional Journalists has a four-point code of ethics, and while memoir writers are not journalists, the part of the Society of Professional Journalist's code called "Minimize Harm" can apply to us. (The code also directs journalists to "Seek Truth and Report It," "Act Independently," and "Be Accountable.") Grief has harmed us, but in writing through our loss, there is no reason to perpetuate that harm.

MY STORY:

I gave my mother a copy of the manuscript of my memoir a few weeks before I sent it in to my publisher. Mom knew that I had been writing it, and we talked often about our memories, sometimes astonished and informed by the different perspectives we brought to the same story: I saw it as a memoir of the deaths of my two sisters and father. To her, the loss was of her two youngest daughters to illness and her husband to instability and divorce.

I wanted to make certain there would be no surprises for her in the book and to give her the opportunity to help me mitigate anything that made her uncomfortable. As a retired magazine editor, she took less than a week to read the more than two hundred loose pages I had bound with a rubber band. When she was done, she called me with one change.

Just one? I was relieved: I knew she had wrestled with how she felt about sharing parts of her private life with strangers. The single scene she objected to involved a depiction of her getting ready for bed and applying face cream. The getting ready for bed part was fine, she said, but I had named the wrong brand of lotion. Please change that, she said. Make sure you name the right brand. My mother used Nivea cream, not Noxzema. Getting that right was important to her, and in the interest of facts and honesty, was important to me.

How the Brain and Body Bargain

Scientists have studied how our brains process information during crises. It turns out that when we perceive that we're in danger, we absorb a lot more sensory information than usual, which is why the world seems to pass by in slow motion when we're under pressure.

Darin Strauss, author of *Half a Life*, gives physical characteristics to the moment of his car accident, not to the car, to himself, or the girl on the bicycle, but to the tragedy itself. He writes,

> This moment has been, for all of my life, a kind of shadowy giant. I'm able, tick by tick, to remember each second before it. . . . But I am powerless to see what comes next; the moment raises a shoulder, lowers its head, and slumps away.

Strauss chose to render the terrible moment as a lurking evil. Something that he, and we, can almost grasp before it slinks out of reach.

Strauss can remember the car accident "tick by tick." I can remember the determined sound of Sarah's voice and her exact words when she told me that I would be "the only one left." Sue William Silverman, who wrote about being sexually abused by her father, saw her life "like snapshots."

Dr. James Pennebaker, a social psychologist who is expert in language use and author of several books, including *Writing to Heal* and *The Secret Life of Pronouns: What Our Words Say About Us* says that as we write about our trauma, we can recall what happened on a more detailed level. Time seems to have slowed down for those moments. "In a car accident or a fall," he told me, "your brain is wide awake, taking in all this information in a way we rarely do." The rest of the time, we don't always retain information in such minute detail.

Dr. Lou Fuerstman, MD, an emergency-care physician, explains that it's also physical: the body focuses in these moments only on what it needs to survive. Inside your system, the stress hormones are moving into "fight or flight" mode.

"There's an internal sense of 'what do I most need to do to survive' and that's correlated with an unusual peak of adrenaline and cortisol," he says. "When something's really threatening to your physical or emotional survival—your sense of who you are—you're getting high levels of stress hormones, which will make you especially focused on what you need, and then doing it. It's not conscious."

When he's writing, Dr. Fuerstman notices that remembering the crisis itself may not be the most important thing. He notes that, "I often don't remember words, but I will remember the feeling of a situation."

Katharine Weber writes of remembering feelings, rather than specific words, in this passage from *The Memory of All That.* Here, she is thirteen, and has been deposited by her father on the Northern California wilderness set of a movie he's involved in.

I got very little sleep those nights on location with Cain's Cut-throats. I didn't dare use the shared bathroom, which required opening closed doors and walking through two rooms in which people were sleeping, and instead crept outside to the dark bushes. I slept in my clothes in the filthy bunkhouse, in the lower bunk of the rickety bunk bed in that partitioned corner. Every night there were different people having sex in the upper bunk. I concluded that they were different people from the sound of their voices, but I had no idea who they were, or how they could think it was okay to have sex in the upper bunk when a thirteen-year-old was sleeping in the bottom bunk. Each night, as the mattress above me bounced rhythmically against the sagging support springs, and the bed frame squeaked, the entire double-decker bed frame rattled and skittered as if we were in steerage quarters on a ship sailing a stormy sea. Though my heart was pounding and I was peculiarly, excruciatingly mortified, I lay very still under my mildewed blanket and pretend to be deeply asleep. I didn't know what else to do.

Weber's father returns for her after five days, and without discussing this incident, they drive to Los Angeles. In this passage, descriptions like "mortified," "sound of their voices," and "pretend" bring the feelings of revulsion, confusion, and anxiety to the forefront in this scene, much more than the names of the characters having sex in the upper bunk or dialogue that the author might have had with her father or with an adult in charge.

As you write through your loss and create a memoir that does justice to your grief and your life, you'll find that bargaining is a lively part of the writing process. As your writing progresses, you will continue to reach agreements with yourself about the ways in which your memories, the research and investigation that you choose to pursue, and even the structure of your true story work together in a memoir that satisfies you.

THE NEXT STEP

1. Using the Hemingway example in this chapter—"For sale: Baby Shoes, Never Worn."—as a starting point,

write a one-sentence story about grief. This sentence can be about anyone's grief.

2. As an example of an uncommon form for a memoir, consider the cookbook or the online recipe site. Try writing your story as a recipe. How would you list the ingredients that go into your story? What would be measured and what requires just "a pinch?" Can you describe what your story would taste like, and to whom you would serve it? Mine might be an entrée to feed a dwindling family. My recipe would include a cup of intellect, a cup of potential, a heaping tablespoon of apprehension, and liberal sprinklings of humor and self-deprecation to taste.

3. Try getting to the heart of your story by crafting a newspaper ad or online notice in which someone is selling something they no longer need or looking for something they don't have. Here's a workshop example derived from a story about a teenager estranged from his mother.

> All dignity must go! We are going out of business and need to sell off batches of self-esteem, self-will, confidence, and more! Contact xyz to inquire about quantities and rates. All sales final. Won't last long!

4. To help place your personal story in the wider world, do research online or in a library about a significant event that matters to you that has taken place during your lifetime, such as the September 11, 2001, attacks, the passage of *Roe v. Wade*, the death of Princess Diana, and so forth. Read newspaper and magazine reports contemporary to the event and use any other primary resource you may have, such as personal memorabilia. Using a double-entry notebook, write on one side of the line the facts about what you have read or examined. On the other side of the line, write your personal experiences,

emotions, and sensory reactions. How does the juxta-position of fact and emotion help you create a scene for your memoir?

5. List the information that you wish you knew for your memoir. Now, separate this into two lists. Put what you can reasonably look up in a library, archive, or other existing research facility into one list, and into a second list, all that you have to put aside for the moment. Comparing the two lists, how much of this "missing" information can you write about in a scenic way if you are clear that you're speculating?

6. Start a brain-spark with this prompt: "If I remembered or knew what I wanted to about (X), I would know (Y) and that would help me write my memoir about my grief because (Z)." Once you've finished, are you still certain that you need that information, or is there another way you can write about what you don't have?

7. Experimenting with pacing can let a reader experience time differently, adding to the emotion of the scene. Try slowing down the action, and write a full page about something that took place in fewer than five minutes. Now, speed up the action, and write one paragraph about a twenty-four-hour period.

8. An interview is just a conversation with a knowledge-able person about a subject you're interested in. Even the busiest people appreciate being asked about their exper-tise. Answer these questions for yourself in order to pre-pare an effective and mutually rewarding interview:

    • Find out everything you can about this person and why their expertise is important to your writing. Be familiar with their current professional reputation and body of work.

    • Prepare a one or two sentence explanation about your memoir in progress that sums up the story and how the expert fits into your writing process. (Take a look at page 230 for help summarizing your story.)

- Make an appointment with the individual, and be prepared to conduct the interview over the phone, in their office, or over a cup of coffee somewhere convenient for you both.
- Confirm the appointment a few days in advance.
- Have at least five and no more than ten questions prepared in order to maximize both of your time. You can confirm information that's readily available, such as a professional title or field of research, but don't ask what you already know or can reliably obtain.
- Take notes or record the interview, but always ask permission. People appreciate knowing that their comments are being taken seriously.
- Allow room for give-and-take conversation and serendipitous turns in topic, but be prepared to get back to the matter at hand.
- Send a thank you note.

Four

DEPRESSION

TAKING CARE OF YOURSELF
WHILE YOU WRITE

Writing honestly through grief involves sadness, of course. You are not trying to undo what happened—that can't be done—but to pursue your understanding of crucial events. You're sad, and you may get depressed. The fourth of Elisabeth Kübler-Ross's five stages is called "Depression," referring to the time when the dying person recognizes the reality of their impending death, and their sadness and grief can make them want to retreat from the world. Cheering someone up when they're truly grieving shortchanges their right to grieve: the grieving person is sad for a reason, and insisting on what might be unrealistic happiness or a brave face deprives him or her of the freedom to express genuine fear or sorrow. This same type of candid assessment also applies to writers crafting their stories of loss.

Rather than use the word "depression," which is a clinical term as well as the flashpoint for both lay and medical opinions about whether or not healthy grief has an expiration date, I'm going to take the liberty of changing the terminology as it applies to writing.

We are troubled, dismayed, even miserable at times. Maybe we've bottomed out (isn't that what a depression is?) or reached a point of stasis. But the desire to write a memoir that addresses loss and grief comes with the understanding that revisiting the emotions connected to that loss is only one part of the bargain. The question becomes not, "Do I run the risk of feeling bad at times as I write?" but "How can I take care of myself as I make this memoir as good as it can be?"

In this section, you will meet writers of grief memoirs who have experienced emotional or physical obstacles in their grieving or their writing. You'll learn about the connection between brain and body, and why the phrase "gut instinct" has a medical basis. Experts will share their knowledge about ways to create productive and healthy periods of distance between you and your memoir-in-progress without abandoning your writing or yourself, and you'll get insight about self-care in emotionally difficult times from a psychologist, an emergency-care physician, and a yoga instructor who specializes in trauma.

Distance Generates Story

The passage of time between the event that caused grief and when the writer feels ready to pick up a pen or open the laptop is one place where your story is found. The person you were then, and the person you are now, create the voices that combine to tell the story.

Social norms or laws may have changed, too, and your own attitudes may have evolved. The more distance you have from your grief, the easier and more gratifying it can be for you to write about it. When I called Dr. James Pennebaker, the social psychologist, to talk about his work, he told me that he has found in his studies that some people have felt they can't write about their grief or trauma because if their writing were discovered, they'd be fired or their spouse would leave them. He told me, "I've had people start off saying, 'if anyone found out, I'd be ruined' and then they write and say it's not a big deal after all. Say you have a trauma when you're fifteen, and if it became public at the time it would be a big deal, but now you're forty years old and you see it's no longer relevant."

When Sue William Silverman was writing her memoir about sexual abuse, she reminded herself that "the hard part had already happened." She knew that she had already survived what had happened to her, and that now she was writing to make sense of the abuse and how her family life as a child had formed her as an adult. She wrote "not to replicate the experience, but to take that experience and turn it into art."

How Writing About Your Grief Makes Healthy Changes

Dr. Pennebaker is interested in what a person's use of words demonstrates about their psychological state. He explained to me that writing about traumatic events creates healthy changes in thought patterns, emotional responses, and sleep and health. Distance from the trauma is good "to the degree that we're able to be honest and stand back and look at things."

In his book *The Secret Life of Pronouns: What Our Words Say About Us*, Dr. Pennebaker explores data about how the words we use show who we are and how we think. Healthy writing, he said, is "characterized by an increasing use of words such as 'because,' 'cause,' 'effect,' 'reason,' and related cognitive words." But he doesn't suggest that a writer of grief memoir stop and evaluate her work on the word-by-word level. In *The Secret Life of Pronouns*, he explains:

Simply requiring people to use the words at a higher rate over the course of writing has no meaningful effects—the writers are simply focusing on words and not their underlying purpose. However, if we encourage people to write about a trauma and work to construct a meaningful story, their writing takes on a more dynamic tone. They begin to stand back and look at their trauma with a broader perspective.

This is what your new—and old—journals and brain-sparks can help you do: find the perspective from which you will tell your story.

Beyond Writing

Ann Hood, who wrote nine novels before her then-five-year-old daughter Grace died suddenly in 2002 of a virulent form of strep, wrote the essay that led to her memoir *Comfort: A Journey Through Grief* two years after her daughter's death. The memoir is about the aftermath of losing her daughter and the ways in which she began to find comfort. "Revisiting the worst time of my life, every day, slayed me," she told me in an email. "But when I saw that I could write beyond my own story . . . I felt it was important to do it."

In this section from *Comfort*, Hood writes in the voice of well-meaning outsiders and then in her own voice, pulling the reader into the futility of their attempts to ease her and the depths of her sorrow.

> Did you know Winston Churchill, Abraham Lincoln, Mark Twain all lost children? And look at what they accomplished! *Then I am not as strong as they were. Grief is bigger than I am.*

Hood writes not only about the devastation to herself and her family after Grace's unexpected death, but about the steps she took, sometimes under the guidance of friends, to help herself cope. Visiting friends, Hood finds that she can't explain her feelings, she can only cry. She writes in *Comfort* about their suggestions and her reactions:

> What a betrayal, I said, to have words abandon me now, when I needed them more than ever.
>
> "Go and learn to upholster a couch!" Hillary said.
>
> I frowned at the suggestions. I was clumsy with needles and thread and had no sense for fabrics or colors.
>
> But they both persisted. "Do something with your hands."
>
> I explained how my hands used to sweat in home economics when it was time to pin the pattern to the fabric; how I snuck home my paisley-print culottes for my cousin to add the zipper; how, during college, in a fit of love and passion, I spent months needle pointing a pillow for a boy. It came out so crooked that I vowed never to waste my time again.

Hood takes up knitting, but in order to knit even a few stitches, she had to concentrate. She explains that, "the magical combination of texture, soothing sound of the needles, and your brain focusing on just one stitch at a time really does have physiological benefits." In an email to me, she pointed out that studies prove that heart rates slow and blood pressure lowers with focused activity, and she suggests that in knitting, she was entering a state "almost like runners or swimmers do." She found relief in an activity where she was *not* grieving.

Dr. Susan O'Doherty, author of *Getting Unstuck Without Coming Unglued: A Woman's Guide to Unblocking Creativity*, who is also a columnist and clinical psychologist, says that while there's not one point in life where grief or trauma feels erased or as if it never happened, writers and others can try to be aware of when they're stepping into a danger zone. "If you get nightmares, if you get sick or start drinking more than usual or relying on prescription or illegal drugs . . . then it's time to step back and look at what we're doing to ourselves and either slow down or seek help getting through it."

When I interviewed her about how writers experience grief as they work, she told me, "writers write until they're written out." Remind yourself to take a walk, to work out at the gym, or do other tasks that aren't directly related to your writing. Schedule those breaks in your daily calendar. It's important to remind yourself to take a walk, go to the gym, and interact with others. Dr. O'Doherty says, "if you're involved in a project that's [emotionally] loaded, it's important to build in a social life as well, because our friends keep us tethered to the present."

Writers want to be open and affected by life, says Kathryn Rhett, author of *Near Breathing: A Memoir of a Difficult Birth,* and editor of the essay collection *Survival Stories: Memoirs of Crisis,* but being open to life also means we can be "open to being wounded and upset." This is true of me when I encounter my sisters' friends, or when a student brings his toddler daughter to the classroom, or a friend tells a joke that I want more than anything to share with Sarah.

Rhett, who has three children, thinks of her house as "a little farm" with two dogs, three cats, and a guinea pig. Taking care of the creatures, she says, is a way of taking care of herself. Walking the dogs and doing family chores keeps her on an even keel. She talks about her work with her husband, novelist Fred Leebron. Having that sense of partnership, along with friends who are writers, is a support system. Rhett suggests that writing other, smaller things like a blog can be a helpful counterpoint to writing a book or constantly tackling difficult subjects.

Grief Memoir and Your Body

You'll find that there are times when you can't write what you had planned to. That day, the topic feels too tender or sore.

Maybe a friend's romantic partner belittles her in a way that reminds you too much of your parents' bad relationship, and as much as you want to write about it, you're too emotionally stirred to do any good work. Make a note in your journal reminding yourself to get to that scene later when you feel ready. Instead, use that writing time for something lighter or less troublesome.

Writing about painful or frightening topics can lead to lack of good nutrition, lack of sleep, even lack of healthy sunlight, says psychologist and author Dr. O'Doherty. A writer might have a day at the computer or pen and pad when nothing's flowing right, the words are stuck or repetitive, or the scene she wants to try to delve into breaks into fragments that scatter out of reach. If you're that writer, you might head to the refrigerator. Bad eating habits, along with lack of sleep or sunlight that can go with writing intensely all have a negative effect on your health as a person and as a writer.

Dr. Fuerstman, an MD, agrees. When people say "my nerves have been rubbed raw," there's a reason. When he and I met to talk about stress and the body, he told me that the ways we normally take care of ourselves are what's needed, but these good habits need to increase when trauma or grief is present. He suggests that you monitor yourself when you feel overwhelmed. Eat right and exercise. He explained that finding an activity that's centering, like meditation, dance, yoga, gardening, or running is helpful. A grieving person should follow "activities that take them to a broader perspective in which they can witness their predicament with more calmness and objectivity."

My bad habits overwhelm my better ones when I'm in the throes of writing emotionally difficult material. My mind won't focus on anything but the world of my writing. My mail goes unopened and my phone messages unanswered. I don't remember to grocery shop; when it's time to make dinner and rejoin the world for the evening, I'll stare into the refrigerator, annoyed that the shelves haven't magically restocked themselves. It's a good thing I'm married to a self-reliant person. Other writers I know confess to eating excessively, hunching over their computers for hours on end, or procrastinating until they're frantic.

There's also a kind of depression that comes after you've finished a draft of your memoir. This project in which you've willingly invested yourself and given so much of your time and attention is coming to a close. You may want to revise your writing later, but for now, that initial, all-consuming push is done. I was surprised to find that when I was done with a full draft of *Invisible Sisters*, I was depressed. After a few days of feeling empty and tearful, I realized that one reason I was upset was that while I wrote, I had spent time, at least in my imagination, with my sisters again. Once the book was completely done I knew I wouldn't be able to do that again in the same way.

It's interesting to consider that when a person grieves a loss in public, friends and family are right there to help. They bring you casseroles, babysit your kids, and arrange ride sharing to the hospital. But when you're grieving again privately and working your way across a page, the caretaking is up to you. Have support systems in place for yourself. Schedule a massage, have fresh flowers on your desk, get outside and stretch. Be your own community with a casserole or a helping hand. When writing gets stressful, walk away for a day, a week, even longer. How long depends on how emotionally "hot" the material is for you. Because writing about grief is willfully approaching a fire that has burned you once, you may find that you are emotionally hurt after writing, and need to heal. You'll know if you're ready to start again when you sit down to rewrite and can make real changes in the work. If you're not seeing any place that needs revision, or are simply moving words around on the page without feeling that you're getting anywhere, you probably haven't given yourself enough time.

MY STORY:

I started practicing yoga more than ten years ago with a group of friends. We met in a cold, crummy loft space that had yet to be "discovered" by realtors. Our teacher was a friend who had studied yoga, our mats were beach towels, and the weekly sessions were energetic, laughter-filled get-togethers that were more like tumbling matches followed by wine. I loved it. That loft building has since gotten HVAC, new windows, and shot out of the price range of many people I know. Most of that group of friends has moved on or moved to distant places. But the yoga stayed with me. I began writing in earnest during that time, and the weekly break to do nothing but concentrate on my otherwise clumsy body and what it could (and could not) do, and the camaraderie of like-minded friends who were also dedicated to taking that weekly break from the work that stressed their days was like a wide open field on a beautiful day.

I started taking yoga classes at a local studio (with actual mats, and teachers who knew that a headstand in your first class is a very bad idea). I'm not athletic, and I'm not thin. I remember sitting down in protest on the hot outfield grass during softball at summer camp. I had no intention of jumping or running to catch a ball. So, I napped, there in the sun with the grasshoppers. Ferdinand the Bull was my literary hero.

Yoga didn't require me to score points. No one shouted distracting trash talk from the sidelines. Other than the yoga teacher's soft voice, the room was quiet, and the music was turned so low it didn't fill my head.

In yoga, I thought only about what was happening at that moment. The more I practiced, the easier it was to get away from my mental gridlock and enjoy what my body was learning to do. The first time I went up into a headstand I opened my eyes and fell right over. Seeing the studio's carpeted floor as the ceiling and the wall with the tapestries and candles upside down unnerved me. It was imperative that I return to how the world had seemed a minute before, when my feet were on the ground where they belonged.

In that headstand, I literally saw my surroundings differently. Once I recognized that and calmed down (the world is *still* right-side up, the cars I see through the window are *not* driving in the air), I went right back into a new headstand. It was analogous to my grief, an upside-down world that I could handle in short intervals.

Doing yoga helped me write through my grief. Every class was ninety minutes I wasn't thinking about what I was writing. I had to think only of my actions in the moment in order to fully appreciate what I was doing on the mat, and in the case of a posture like a headstand, to stay safe. And yet, seeing the world differently in that headstand helped my writing, because I experienced what it felt like to see the world a new way, which was what I had intended for myself in writing through loss.

Amy Weintraub is an internationally recognized yoga teacher who specializes in yoga for depression and anxiety. She recommends a regular yoga practice for writers dealing with grief or trauma, and explained when we talked that yoga can help a writer understand that you can, "have this story about what happened to me or my loved ones . . . but I am so much more than that." In her book *Yoga Skills for Therapists: Effective Practices for Mood Management,* Weintraub writes about studies that have shown yoga's positive effect on the brain, enabling people to learn and grow from their experiences. Just breathing can affect your mood. Anxious people tend to take short breaths. She writes "taking just one deep breath uses more of your lungs than you may been using the moment before. In that instant, you are bringing more oxygen into your system, feeding your brain."

Take a deep breath, and revise your manuscript when you're ready.

The Ritual of the Nice Notebook

Kathryn Rhett is serious about her notebooks. She writes in her university office and at home, but for her, it's crucial to always carry a spiral notebook with a pocket for photos or interesting cards. She says that the notebook is "like a garden that has to be fertilized. I have to fill it with interesting things. Asking myself what I think about [those things] gets me into the act" of writing.

Rhett feels that picking the right notebook is a ritualistic act involving choice. She likes her "humble" office-supply store spiral pocket notebook, college ruled.

I used to protest that I didn't have any writing rituals. And then I caught myself rearranging my writing studio so that I could look out the window into the backyard from my desk, because no other view felt quite right. I couldn't write as well if I faced a wall or the door. And then I noticed that I was selective about my notebooks, too. For me, they're best if they're unlined pages, eight and half by eleven inch paper, with no decoration on the hard cover. This way, I can write top to bottom, draw or paint, or clip mementos onto the pages without feeling constrained by lines.

The knowledge that you have your own notebook, just the way you like it, can stave off that feeling of being stuck and sad. In my case, so can the sight of my cat sleeping on the reading chair in my studio, untouched by depression or sadness, pleased only with the brown corduroy cushion and his view of the yard.

The Dangers of Emotional Stress

Stress can make you sick. You've surely heard this, but there is medical science behind the warning. Revisiting trauma and grief can be stressful, even when you're prepared and know that the memoir you're writing will have emotionally difficult moments. Dr. Lou Fuerstman says that the relationship between brain and body is complex. Looking back at a stressful situation tends to create stress in the present moment, he told me, which can lead to an increase in the body's production of the stress hormones cortisol and epinephrine. This can throw the immune system out of balance, which can lead to increased susceptibility to infections like a cold or flu, or in other cases, to autoimmune diseases like some types of arthritis or diabetes.

Marianne Leone grew ill after her son Jesse's death, and writes about the experience in her memoir. She grew weak, rejected the taste of food, and, at her husband's urging, despite her reluctance to deal with doctors after her son's experiences, went for an exam, and found that she had a tumor that weighed what her son had weighed at birth, a "three-and-a-half pound Rorschach blot from the planet Rage 'n' Grief." Her surgery was successful; the cancer had not spread.

"I was in such spiritual and psychic pain that I didn't feel connected to my body," she told me. "I feel like my body said 'enough!'" Writing an essay about her son for *The Boston Globe* just a few months after he died felt to her "like lancing something that allowed me to breathe and write."

In my case, when I came home from staying with our mother for the month after Sarah's death, I thought I was doing better, although I had a cold I couldn't shake. My congestion became bronchitis, but I went to work every day, sick as I was, until I passed out with a high fever one morning at home. A friend took me to the doctor, and the doctor sent me home to bed with a diagnosis of pneumonia.

I felt as if I were coughing rocks. I slept for what seemed

like weeks. Grief had laid me low and my body was attempting of its own accord to emulate what Shakespeare wrote for Macbeth: knit up the raveled sleeve of care.

One day I woke craving pancakes, although I'm not normally a fan. In my rumpled pajamas, with bed head and I'm sure looking for all the world like a person who had been in a daze pretty much an entire month, I savaged my pantry and somehow found a questionably dated box of pancake mix. And I made pancakes as if my life depended on it. And then I sat at my dining room table and devoured the stack. I'm sure it was late in the day: I had been sleeping almost around the clock.

And when I was done, I was exhausted. The act of making pancakes and eating them was Herculean, and I could barely clear the table. As I recall, I rinsed the dishes and staggered back to bed, where I slept, apparently fortified by starch, water, sugar, and reconstituted blueberries, for several more days.

The shock of my sister's death, caring for our mother, neglecting to care for myself, and finally returning to a demanding job as if nothing was wrong had taken its toll on me, sending me to bed, miserable and sick, for a long time.

Grief Writers in the World

One way to take care of yourself when you're in the throes of writing a memoir about loss is to make time for an activity that heals others, like volunteering for a cause that's important to you. To Dr. Susan O'Doherty, meaningful human interaction can be a kind of insurance against depression. For survivors of trauma, she says, "it's human nature to blame ourselves when things go wrong, even if we really had no control over what happened. We all want to feel like we're in control of circumstances, because it's a way of assuring ourselves that it's not going to happen again."

Loading boxes at a food kitchen, walking dogs at a shelter, or answering the phones at a fund drive reminds you, even as you're in the deepest trenches of revisiting your own grief, that life, with all its dark and light, is still going on.

MY STORY:

In the weeks after Hurricane Katrina, when more than a quarter of a million people relocated to cities across the United States, including my home, Atlanta, I volunteered at a shelter and food kitchen that assisted the displaced. I wrote about the experience in my journal, and tried hard to capture small details that I might forget if I didn't put them on paper.

> Here's what I learned about what we would need if we were ever evacuees. Our social security cards and driver's licenses, to register for benefits. Lots of underwear. A hat and an umbrella, for waiting hours in the sun. Packaged wipes or clean-up cloths. Books, because of the long waits. What to have when I volunteer? A place to stash my purse. Pockets. Patience. With about twenty other people, I sorted plastic garbage bags of donated clothing onto long tables in the parking lot. Infant, toddler, men, women. We started a table of footwear and dug through big cardboard boxes of shoes in the sun, matching pairs, looking for pairs. . . . I ended up opening boxes of diapers—who knew diapers came in sizes?—we made a chain of boxes, labeling them "newborn," "3–6 months" up to twenty-four months.

> The importance of volunteering wasn't new to me. One of the many good things I carry with me from my upbringing, brought into even sharper focus by the grief of losing

so much of my family, is the value of social justice and what in Hebrew is called *tikkun olam,* or repair of the world.

This chance to help out came along while I was struggling with how tumultuous I felt writing about my own loss and with the huge time commitment of writing a book while working as a freelance writer. My "fight or flight" responses had been activated by my own writing; that same reaction that alerted a prehistoric human to run if he heard a saber-toothed tiger roar in the distance. The beast has attacked before, and here it comes again. My stress hormones were in overdrive. I didn't chide myself about taking time away from the manuscript. My gut told me that I needed a break from my emotionally threatening writing.

"Gut" reactions have earned their name. "There's a reality to the 'gut' reaction," Dr. Fuerstman said when we spoke about stress and the body. "The autonomic nervous system has a network of nerves in the viscera—the gut— and they communicate with each other with the same neurotransmitters that the brain does. There are areas that help make complex decisions unconscious." Which means, as yoga teacher Amy Weintraub told me, "we can trust intuition."

If your intuition tells you to take time away from your writing because you need the perspective that distance gives or, or if you're not feeling well emotionally or physically, trust yourself. If you're anxious to keep writing, work for the time being on scenes that aren't as emotionally potent. Turn to your journal and write there. Or put everything aside that seems to you to be related to your writing about grief, and go for a walk, cook a meal, see your friends, or help someone else out. When you return to the page, you'll hopefully find that the emotional or physical stasis has receded.

When Writing Is a Thicket

Some people compare writing to gardening: planting ideas as seeds, nurturing their gentle growth as the words become abundant, brilliant flowers. Others sometimes feel that they're hacking through a thicket, cutting away overgrowth to find the path that they know is somewhere in the woods. Here, in a passage near the halfway point of her memoir, Marianne Leone writes about how demanding writing her memoir can be.

> I am hacking at the reeds again today, which is what I do the days I can't conjure Jesse for this book. I have been trying to call Jesse back to a place where he's alive and five years old and eager to learn about the world around him, but instead I keep finding him dead in his bed. So I stand in the thicket of the parasitic reeds that are taking over the tidal marsh behind my house and I hack at them ineffectually with a giant pincer tool. . . . [T]he reeds tower over me, ten feet tall. They sway mockingly as I cut them once, twice, three times, until they are only two feet high. Then I stomp their stems down, the most satisfying and rewarding part of this ritual.

Cutting the reeds, she finds a dead bird, and is reminded of herself at six years old, finding a dead bird and learning that it couldn't be revived.

> Finding the bird is the long way to come back to Jesse. Trying to summon him, I was hurled into that moment when his stillness signaled an end and not sleep . . . I don't need to be reminded that Jesse is dead, or that on the day preceding the night he died a bird slammed into the sliding glass door a few feet from where he sat. . . . I have to keep going, to see if I can summon another place, another time,

when he was alive. I turn my back on the bird and hack again at the reeds, cutting them down to raise Jesse up.

In this scene, Leone struggles with an overgrowth of reeds, and by attacking them, she sees herself trying to gain control of the images that crowd her writing mind. Your own depression or stagnation in your writing can seem like trying to see your way through a tangle of images, emotions, and stories. You might feel angry or lost, want to start over, or quit altogether. This might be a good time to get some distance and edit what you've written so far, hacking away at the overgrowth to reestablish a clear view of your goal: an honest and well-written memoir of your grief and the way that loss has affected your life.

Avoiding the Hard Stuff

You can also get depressed if you're frustrated or displeased with what you've written so far. Reading your memoir may bring on surprising emotions, even as you've learned to think of your story of grief with distance and a critical eye. Reimagining an encounter with a difficult person in order to write about them can make you almost as gloomy as the first time they came into your life (although now you have the benefit of distance in knowing how the interaction turned out). There might be days when your writing itself is frustrating: the right words escape you, or a particular piece of information that you feel you need just isn't available.

If what you've written feels empty or disengages you, you can trust your intuition here, too. You may simply have spent a little too much time in the company of your own work and need a break. If writing becomes a chore, or if reading through what you've written so far means that you'd rather read yesterday's coupon flyer, now might be the time to inspect your writing for places where you've put up a safety shield.

A safety shield works like the thick plastic window between the cashier and the customer in some convenience stores and in taxicabs. The plastic is scratched and blurry, and although it's there for a good reason, the protection it offers keeps one side from communicating clearly with the other. The transaction gets completed after a few tries, but no one makes a personal connection. In a grief memoir, that shield keeps you from your readers and from yourself.

You can start dismantling the safety shield by looking for a few things. If you are writing "around" what you really want to say, you're probably avoiding a subject or an image because you're worried that it might trouble you or someone else. A dull sentence or a vague description might mean that you're pulling your hand away too soon. You might be "clearing your throat" on the page, like a nervous speaker at an awards banquet, writing about what you'll tell us and how you'll tell it, but postponing the heart and soul of the scene itself.

> TIP: Don't write something that will truly hurt too badly to recover from, but trust your intuition to tell you if your resistance to writing is because you're genuinely concerned that the idea you're following will lead to emotional or physical reinjury, or if you're just nervous about burning yourself emotionally. You can always try to write that difficult scene, knowing that you can stop if the writing stirs up trouble that's not useful for you or the memoir.
>
> Another way that your writing will show if you're writing around your topic is if you lean too far toward the "I" perspective without placing the protagonist—you—in the larger world. You've left the reader unsure about with whom that "I" is interacting, and why. Maybe your writing is still missing an element of research or a contrasting point of view. Without these, your characters and setting might not be portrayed as fully as they can be.
>
> Perhaps you're giving in to the volume of your emotions and overwriting. Embellishing your sentences obscures the

impact that a simpler statement could make. Mark Twain, known for his biting wit, wrote, "If you catch an adjective, kill it." Every modifier doesn't need to be relegated to the trash pile, but one can be a nice touch.

An overwritten passage can detach a reader as quickly as a lackluster one. A woman whose adult daughter had died unexpectedly could no longer shop at the grocery store she was accustomed to, because her daughter had shopped there, too. "I kept expecting to see her on the other side of the broccoli display," she told me. Her conversational description has immediate impact in its frankness about the way grief traps us in the most mundane places. Dressing up her sentence and the idea behind it would rob the statement of its power. Another simple way to write it might be to write that her grief *ambushed* her over the broccoli. Simplicity gets crushed as the embellishment gets thicker. A phrase like "her grief popped up like an *animatronic monster* at a theme park" obscures the purity of the writing. A phrase like "her grief *ambushed* her over the *lumpy green* broccoli that *towered in mountainous piles, like a sparkle-eyed, fanged, evil animatronic monster* at a theme park ride" completely demolishes the emotion and meaning. The best and most honest way to write about that grief would be with the same simplicity as she said it.

Journalist Janny Scott has a "bias for understatement" in writing. To her, anything beyond understatement feels cloying. As one of the many *New York Times* writers contributing to that paper's "Portraits of Grief" series, Scott captured details about the victims of the September 11th attacks in daily stories that typically ran no longer than about three hundred words. As she interviewed family members about their missing loved ones in the frantic days following the disaster, she says that her scalp would tingle when she heard the "telling detail" about her subject that would make them memorable to a reader who didn't know them.

> TIP: That kind of telling detail lives in the inscription inside a
> wedding ring, a long-awaited letter that arrives a day too late,
> or a missed train connection that changes a life. For me, some
> of the telling details in grief memoirs that I can never forget
> are in *The Year of Magical Thinking*. In that memoir, Joan
> Didion writes of looking at her husband's driver's license
> when she's asked about donating his organs. He wore
> eyeglasses, and her phrase, "his blue imperfect eyes," is an
> achingly loving comment that makes my hair stand on end.
> Similarly, the way Lucy Grealy, in *Autobiography of a Face*,
> describes the sensation of chemotherapy invading her body
> as an "anatomy lesson" has never left me. What can you write
> that makes your own hair stand on end? Discard the writing
> that bores you. Put the weaker material in your "kill your
> darlings" folder to rewrite another time.

In Michael Steinberg's memoir, *Still Pitching*, his attention
to detail is one of the craft techniques that makes the story universal. Not everyone plays baseball, or was a teenage boy in
New York in the fifties. But every adult was a teenager once,
and it's Steinberg's use of physical and emotional detail that
makes the commonality clear to the reader. On the nominal
level, he writes about his love for baseball while growing up in
New York in the 1950s and '60s. On a deeper level, the memoir
explores his identity as a Jew and as a teenager strategizing his
way through the humiliation of wanting to play baseball and being relegated, at first, to the demeaning role of gofer. On an even
deeper level, the memoir addresses the frustration that teenag-
ers feel in nearly anything they try to do in the adult world.
And that's a connection with the reader.

In this section from *Still Pitching*, in which Steinberg is a
high school sophomore called to that coach's office, each detail
is noteworthy.

The room was a ten-foot-square box, a glorified cubby-
hole, smelling of Wintergreen, Merthiolate, and stale

sweat socks. The chipped, brown cement floor was coated with dust and rotted out orange peels. On all four sides, makeshift two-by-four equipment bays overflowed with old scuffed helmets, broken shoulder pads, torn jerseys and pants. Muddy cleats and deflated footballs were piled haphazardly on top of one another.

Mr. K. stood under a bare light bulb wearing a blue baseball hat, white sweat socks, and a jock strap. He was holding his sweatpants and chewing a plug of tobacco. "You're Steinberg, right?" He said the name, "Stein-berg" enunciating and stretching out both syllables.

"I don't beat around the bush, Stein-berg. You're here for one reason and one reason only."

Coach K. offers him a post as assistant football manager, not a spot on the baseball team. Disappointed that he'd been pegged as a "glorified water boy" and that the coach might have been asked as a favor to bring him on, Steinberg struggles with the decision to accept:

I was numb with humiliation.

Notice how the author uses the words "broken," "torn," and "deflated" in his descriptions of the equipment in the coach's office. He's describing what he saw, and allowing us to see with him as we read his words. He is also indicating how the character of Mike Steinberg, the teenager, feels in the presence of the coach.

At first, Steinberg says, he just wrote what happened, and then what happened after that. When he went back through what he remembers now as hundreds of pages of notes, he saw that he'd written about something deeper. "I had this coach I hadn't thought about for about thirty years, not even an inkling, he didn't factor into anything to do with me or my life, but he appeared every three or four pages" in the notes. "Once I got to the twelfth or so mention of him, I threw everything out that wasn't him."

* * *

The poet Robert Frost wrote in his essay, "The Figure a Poem Makes," that if there were no tears in the writer, there would be none in the reader. He extended this to say that surprise for the writer would surprise the reader. For me, that means that if you're not honest enough in your own writing to make yourself cry—and for those of us who write about grief, that means cry again as we take ourselves back to those times and places—your emotion and meaning won't have an impact on the reader. The same goes for the surprises in writing: your satisfaction in recognizing meaning that you had overlooked or hadn't been ready to see comes through to the reader, along with your joy in finding that you have the ability to look back and smile, or even laugh.

MY STORY:

That moment of surprise for me makes me want to run around my studio with my hands in the air like a winning prizefighter. "I just remembered the time that Sarah and I tried to break into our house because I forgot the keys," I might want to shout, and then, "Oh my gosh, this is also a connection with my metaphor for investigating the damaged body!"

Of course there are tears, too, There were terrible tears that came and went during the time I wrote my memoir. Going through a folder where I'd stored some of Susie and Sarah's early ephemera—drawings, birthday cards, and the like—I found a handmade storybook. The crayon drawings were both careful and awkward, as little kids' artwork always is. Susie had written and illustrated a pamphlet-sized book she called "Mrs. Spider and the Giant" for Sarah, who was then too young to read. In the story, a lady spider sets sail on a raft made of twigs, heading for a better life. In her new land, she befriends a giant. And, because it's a kids' story, everyone lives happily ever after.

The last page of Susie's book reads:

I have two things for you today. One I made two
days ago and I lost it and found it again and one I
made today. I will make you some words and write
them the best I can.
Love, Susie.

Under that is a line so straight that it must have been
made against a ruler, and then Sarah's early attempts at
writing.

Sarah LOVE.

This page made me weep until my stomach hurt. I
found the folder in the early evening, and when my husband came home from work he found me crying, freshly
heartbroken again. We had plans with friends that night,
and he offered to cancel for us. I wanted to go, I told him.
I'd stop crying soon.

Time had shifted with his arrival home. I wanted very
much to be in my present-day life again, and I put the
drawing back in the folder. I stopped crying, but my stomach hurt all night.

I photocopied the original page, framed it, and hung
it on my studio wall. Yes, it hurts to see it there. But it
would hurt worse not to.

When Janisse Ray reads aloud from her memoir *Ecology
of a Cracker Childhood*, she says that "even after having read
[pieces] hundreds of times aloud in public, I can still feel
the same emotions they were written with. Maybe it was
written with such emotion that it can never be separated."

But experiencing strong emotion as you write—tears
or joy—doesn't necessarily translate directly to the page.
Monotony, for the reader or for the author, can still set in,
and that calls for rewriting.

Rewriting means critically reviewing what you've written so far. If you parse the word "review" as "view again," rewriting means that you're viewing your writing a second, third, fourth, or even more times. When you revise, you're looking for much more than typographical and grammatical errors. You're grooming your work to make sure that coherence, consistency, and crucial imagery do the work you intend for them to do. Style matters in revision, too. It doesn't matter if your voice on the page is loving and thoughtful, like John Bayley's in *Elegy for Iris*, his memoir of his wife Iris Murdoch's fading from Alzheimer's disease, or conversational and direct, like Sonya Huber's *Cover Me: A Health Insurance Memoir*. If the voice feels right to you, that's not what you want to revise. Instead, take a look at the way the memoir's plot flows. Read your sentences aloud and listen carefully to determine if they have the meaning and the rhythm that you intend. And most of all, ask yourself if your memoir looks at the little things that make your story yours alone.

Adjust Your Focus to See the Little Things

Grief is large and shape-shifting, and the feelings that accompany great loss are hard to pin down. Sadness itself changes shape and size from day to day. By writing the small and sometimes seemingly irrelevant details of your own grief or loss, you bring the big-picture view into focus for yourself as plot, scene, imagery, character, and dialogue. Once you've adjusted your vision this way, your larger narrative is clearer to you, and easier to write about.

For example, Neil White wrote in *In the Sanctuary of Outcasts* about how his experience in prison caused him to reflect on his life and change it. To serve that story, he adjusted his focus to write about the crime that sent him to prison, and the depth of loss he felt in being away from his wife and small children. He wrote very little about parts of his life that didn't relate directly to that narrative. In *A Three Dog Life*, Abigail Thomas writes primarily about her husband's accident and its effect on their marriage, even though we know from her other work and her voice on the page that she has plenty of stories to tell. The story of the entirety of your life so far is the biggest and toughest darling to kill to when you're writing memoir. That summer at camp may not matter in your plot, even though it is a part of your past.

As you write, you'll naturally be sad and even stuck sometimes if you continue to write in a way that's honest with yourself and your readers. But sadness doesn't have to be constant or halt your writing altogether. Knowing how to recognize when to take a break, how to care for yourself physically and emotionally, and how to measure if your sadness adds to your writing or if you've gone too far are the hallmarks of a grieving writer moving forward toward renewal.

THE NEXT STEP

1. Write something that scares you, that's "too" honest or sad or angry, that you don't believe you would ever use in your memoir. Put that writing away where you're not tempted to reread it or revise. Look at it again in a month. Do you still feel the same way about it?

2. An edit as simple as placing the right verb in the right place snaps a scene into sharp focus. Take a scene that you've already written (or write one for this exercise) in which two characters in your memoir interact, using their bodies in some way. Perhaps they are fighting, gesturing across a room, making love, exercising, or engaging in physical therapy. Now try to up the ante on at least

one verb in each sentence, so that the action conveys increased emotion and meaning. For example, "cry" might become "wail," or "stare" might become "glare." Refer to a thesaurus, a dictionary, a favorite poem, or another memoir to unearth verbs you might not think of right away. Take care not to overwrite or make things up.

3. Write about a physical change in you since you began grieving. Perhaps you fell ill or got injured, or became newly committed to exercise or study. How and why was the physical change related to your grief? Write a scene in which that physical change is the focus of your character's attention.

4. Grief is hard to pinpoint on the page. It's an abstract concept that shifts in our lives from day to day. Sue William Silverman says of abstractions that, "in a way, [a writer should] avoid the word 'grief.'" Try to write a paragraph about your grief that doesn't use the word "grief." Avoid direct synonyms like "loss" or "hurt." Be as concrete and specific as you can in writing about what the grief feels like, looks like, or how it manifests in you or others.

5. Give yourself some physical distance from your memoir and see what develops. Get up from the desk. Shut off your computer or close your notepad. Trade one of your writing sessions for a "not-writing" session. Instead, engage yourself in the life you're leading now. Take a walk. Participate in a sport, go to a concert, a gallery, or out with friends to talk about something other than writing or loss. Make a special trip to a farmer's market or buy fresh groceries, and cook an interesting meal. When you return to the hard work of writing about your grief, you'll feel refreshed.

Five

ACCEPTANCE

ADDING NEW CHAPTERS TO YOUR LIFE

By now you know that writing about grief doesn't mean shutting the door on grief once you're done with a first draft, or washing your hands of what has happened to you and then wiping it away forever. Writing about your grief helps you move toward a point in your life where although loss isn't gone, it no longer blocks your progress. "We're never done," author Sue William Silverman told me about the idea of "closure." "I don't want [my emotions] to be done," she continued, "that's the irony of it. Closure is a form of death [and] I always want to look at experience from a different angle." Other writers who have experienced grief agree: Dani Shapiro writes in *Devotion: A Memoir,* her story of spiritual and emotional self-assessment, that closure, while a seductive idea, is a "myth."

Your memoir demonstrates to you and to those who will read your writing that you have accepted grief as one of many parts of your ongoing life. You've written about your loss in a way that places your initial experience with your loss in the past, recognizing that your grief is a factor that's shaped you while you continue living your own story, your ongoing life. Having written about what you've lost and how it's changed, you shine light on your future. You've already done the hardest part, which is surviving the loss itself. And now you've done the second hardest part, which is writing the story of that loss.

It's ironic that in order to write well about our own grief, we have to look beyond it. The fifth stage in the Kübler-Ross model is "Acceptance," when a dying person comes to terms with their mortality, or when a grieving person begins to understand that living after loss must become their normal state of being. For you, writing the true story of your grief, "Acceptance" is the point at which you see your story on the page as both separate from and integral to your life experience. Now that you have your story on paper, you can begin to measure how your loss has shaped your approach to your own next chapters. Think back to the concept of reader reward and writer reward. You've now made it to writer reward: the sometimes understated or even unexpected pride that comes from capturing the story of a life or a place, or in seeing yourself as the survivor.

As readers, we're drawn to grief memoirs because we want to know how the author made it through. You've written your memoir because you want to know what you did or said or believed that helped *you* make it through. You've reached the part in writing that memoir where you put your pin in the plot map past the "yes, and . . . ," and appreciate yourself and what you've done. You've written about your loss in a form that puts you in a position to see that even though you may not have recognized it until you began writing, you're looking ahead.

In this section, you will gather tools that will help you enjoy and accept your growing writing craft as you've applied it to your difficult story. You'll learn ways to give yourself good advice about continuing to shape your work. You'll also get tips for using the brain-spark as an ongoing part of your life as a writer.

Coming to Terms with Your Story

"People often told me that I should write a memoir," Paul Guest says. Friends and family knew his story: that he had broken his neck in a bicycle accident when he was twelve and his life was forever changed. "This was extremely dramatic for anyone to hear. It was evocative and telling to them, but for me at some point it became ancient history," he says. "I had to go on with my life. I couldn't be terribly sad every day of my life."

Guest remembers a professor in a college poetry class questioning him about a line he had written in a poem about shaving in a mirror. "Why didn't I say that someone else's hands were shaving my face?" he remembers her asking. At first, he says he resisted making that change in what he'd written, but, he told me, "life is the sum total of everything that happens to you." Denying or ignoring a wound that you carry, physically or emotionally, "isn't necessarily honest or fruitful."

Author and social psychologist Dr. James Pennebaker observes that, "it's often threatening to tell a deeply personal story." But one of the reasons we tell stories is because, "humans naturally need to understand complex experiences. [P]utting it into words helps you come to terms with it."

MY STORY:

I didn't realize that I had come to accept what had happened to my family and to me until I was deep in the process of writing my memoir. I was nearly done, in fact, when an image came to me. I wrote about it this way:

> I first noticed that I had arrived at my life in progress when I caught myself talking in [my] empty kitchen. I lived alone: I was addressing myself. The act of talking to myself wasn't what

startled me. What startled me was that I was happy.

This scene occurs toward the end of the memoir. I had, in what was my present-day life, been renovating my kitchen, peeling away old wallpaper while standing on a chair under a naked bulb. A metaphor emerged from the hands-on process of fixing up my house. I got down from the chair, found a pad and pen, and wrote, expanding on one of the brain-sparks that shed light I was determined to see by.

There was no single moment when I made the choice not to cave in: I just stayed upright and held on. I held on in Los Angeles, warming my skin under the beachy glare. I held on at my mother's house the day of Sarah's funeral, when I confronted my father for leaving me. I held on when I bought the headstone for Susie's grave, and I held on during a summer night in Atlanta, peeling grease-spattered wallpaper printed with smiling teapots from my kitchen walls.

I had come to accept that I had arrived at my life in progress. I didn't then, and never will shrug off my sisters' lives and their deaths, or my father's, and say that they don't matter. Writing about all of these things held them in my sight line, and made me examine them and feel their heat. When I look away from the fire, I'm all the more aware of how much I want my life in progress to mean. My grief hasn't left me, and I can't undo what caused it. What I can do is continue to write about my memories, our family's story, and about the woman who is me now, both happy and sad, forged from that grief.

Learn to Trust Yourself

As you write what feels best on a particular day, you may worry about being sure that you've gotten your history correct, or about pleasing everyone involved in the story. Feeling uneasy about your writing might make you want to skip over material that's important to you. You might be concerned about making sure that you write in a way that presents your grief and your current life convincingly without sounding self serving or self indulgent. Another worry on a long list might be about how people will respond when they learn you're writing a book, and how they might react if it's published.

Just keep writing. Remind yourself that at this stage you're only putting words on paper. No one but you has to see them. You already know that you're dedicated to crafting your story in such a way that the people you love never question your motives. Keep that in mind, and your list of worries will shrink.

Rolling the File Cabinet Aside

Your brain isn't a file cabinet. That image is too basic to represent the complexities of how a brain works. But try to imagine memories, facts, images, and questions about your loss as the loose files, papers, and paraphernalia sticking willy-nilly out of a heavy, beige, metal four-drawer cabinet. Before you wrote about your grief, that cabinet blocked your way forward in life—you couldn't get around that huge obstacle. Writing about your loss doesn't discard the cabinet, but writing organizes the files and rolls the cabinet to the side. Sometimes you will roll it all the way behind you so that it's no obstruction at all. You have written a draft of your memoir, and your loss no longer blocks your way.

TIP: Can you locate a moment or several moments in your story when you recognized that you had changed? What are specific actions that you do in your life now to commemorate the people, places, or skills that you grieve? These images may be the sources for scenes that continue to move your memoir forward to its conclusion and the implied new beginning.

MY STORY:

Just a few years ago, a cousin with whom I'm close told me over dinner at her house that she had never known exactly what was wrong when we were kids, only that my sisters—her young cousins—were very sick.

Suddenly inspired, she left the table to fetch some photographs. She showed her teenage daughter a snapshot of her, me, and Susie as little girls, dressed in nineteen-sixties high-style "mod" formal wear for a family wedding. Reminiscing about our white lace minidresses, we explained to her daughter that the littlest girl in the picture, with the dark curly hair and the big grin, was Susie. We started to patch together bits of information about what my cousin had heard from her parents (almost nothing, because they were told almost nothing) with what I knew from firsthand experience.

My habit had been to tell only the bare bones and spare the listener, but now that my memoir was written and I had allowed myself to feel comfortable expressing my love for my family, along with my laughter and my anger (those mixed emotions again), I could see how the people I remembered so well could also become whole again to a listener. My cousin's daughter asked questions; her mother and I laughed and argued and remembered our own versions of our stories as we answered her.

You Have Permission to Laugh

"You can only bear the hard stuff for so long," Ethan Gilsdorf says. He didn't intend his memoir to be a "five-hanky" read, so his self-deprecating humor plays a large part in his tone in *Fantasy Freaks and Gaming Geeks*. "We don't need laugh-out-loud memoirs about loss, but I remember the crazy scenes we had at home," he says, recalling the time his mother threw a buttered roll at the television, aiming for Julia Child. If handled honestly and with respect, humor can bring air and light to a grief memoir, particularly if you're the kind of person who sees the irony or humor in a tough situation. Humor, if it's genuine, diffuses a tough situation.

Author and editor Dinty W. Moore regularly brings his quick wit to his writing. In his memoir, *Between Panic and Desire*, he's irreverent about growing up in the sixties and seventies, but his joking reveals some serious contemplation about the meaning of manhood in our culture. In chapter six, "Questions and Activities Before Continuing" (chapter eleven has the same title and a different set of questions) Moore writes:

1. Which of the following would you advocate as an appropriate replacement father for the author of this memoir:
    a. Hugh Beaumont
    b. Hugh Brannum
    c. A big plastic baggie of aromatic marijuana
    d. Twenty-five years of cognitive therapy
    e. All of the above

An arresting approach to the absence of a father, don't you think? In talking about why he wrote that scene, Moore compares a list like this one to a pop fly in baseball. "The best punch lines are short, and humor often catches a reader off guard," he says. He explains that humor can introduce a reader to difficult truths about human nature, about sexuality, illness, or other topics from which they otherwise might shy away. He told me that "what art does best is surprise people and startle them into thinking about things. You can do that with an unexpected bit of humor, [and get] the reader to jump outside of the groove and think 'oh, there are other ways to think about this.'"

Marianne Leone says of her son, who lived with cerebral palsy until his death at the age of seventeen, "I knew [Jesse] was intelligent, because grasping humor is a sign of intelligence." At eight months old, he was laughing to the sped-up sounds of Alvin and the Chipmunks. Her voice, witty and acerbic, comes through in this section from *Knowing Jesse* about a caregiver's mishap and Jesse's appreciation for slapstick comedy.

> Brandy got to know Jesse on her first week with us via some dog vomit. Jess and Brandy were watching television while Chris and I were on a date night. Brandy got up for something and sat down heavily in the overstuffed green chair. Jess clicked his "kiss" sound urgently and inclined his head toward Brandy.
> "What is it Jesse? Are you thirsty?"
> Another urgent click and head bob.
> "You're thirsty."
> A headshake. No.
> "You're not thirsty?"
> Another click. Head bob.
> "What is it? Okay, I'll get the computer."
> Jess watched her intensely, holding his breath. Brandy put her hand down, stood up, looked down, and saw she had been sitting in a pool of Goody's [the dog] vomit. Jesse laughed, delighted. A seven-year-old's dream come true!

Leone heard the story from Brandy, and retold it in her memoir.

Writing the funny moments adds depth to the characters, and shines a light on their real traits: in this scene, a little boy who, like all little boys, revels in gross jokes. And the reader and the author both laugh, the weight of grief lifted, at least for a moment.

> **TIP:** A brain-spark on the subject of a particular conversation from the past can jog your memory for funny moments. Ask yourself one key question about the conversation you're trying to remember before you start. If you're writing about a friend from college days whom you wish you could reconnect with, try asking yourself something unique to your relationship with him, like "What was that crazy phrase he always used that made us laugh so hard?" To put yourself in the mind-set to remember, you might want to play one of your favorite songs from that era. You may want to notice how your body feels and which emotions you're experiencing when you let yourself remember. Agitation, laughter, even ruefulness may be what brings the scene back to you. In this way, you're allowing yourself to accept that the current state of loss, as well as the warm feelings you had about a friendship or conversation when it happened, both belong in your story.

MY STORY:

My sister Sarah and I were both fans of the band the Grateful Dead. (Do what you will with the name, I choose to believe our attraction was to the music, not the moniker.) There's a tradition at Grateful Dead concerts for would-be attendees who don't have tickets. They wander outside the venue before the show with their forefingers pointed skyward, repeating the phrase "I need a miracle." What they mean is they need a single ticket.

Sarah's death was unexpected when it happened, although we knew she would die young. No gravesite had been purchased, no memorial preplanned. And so when my mother and I sat in the funeral director's office the day after Sarah's death, he made several phone calls to locate a single available gravesite, ideally in the same cemetery as my mother's parents were interred on Boston's South Shore.

As my mother and I watched him, my sudden urge to hold my forefinger to the sky and chant, "I need a miracle" startled me. Even though I was shocked and brokenhearted at my sister's death and reeling from the stress involved in arranging her funeral, the sudden image of a lonely fan outside a rock concert nearly made me laugh. And oddly, I knew it would have made Sarah laugh, too—the idea of this somber moment disrupted by what we would both agree was a perverse insider's joke.

Humor is strange and sometimes private: the "in-joke" that only a few people will get, the slapstick humor that makes some people weep with joy and others with misery. Professions have their own jokes—do you ever wonder what a rocket scientist says instead of "it's not rocket science"? Humor is a slippery thing; what's funny to one person may be offensive or simply fall flat to another. There's a kind of bravery in writing about those radiant moments of humor that occurred before or even during a time of sorrow. We've learned to hang our heads in the presence of loss, but in celebrating a loved one or a happy time, sometimes that person's favorite joke is a perfect way to write them fully onto the page. If you're unsure about the tone of a funny item that you've included in your memoir, read the passage aloud, or share it with another reader and gauge their reactions.

TIP: Allowing humor into your writing about grief lets you and your readers experience an emotionally charged moment from another angle. That change in perspective benefits your writing by adding depth to the scene and varying the mood or tone of the memoir as a whole. In using humor, you're signaling to yourself that you've accepted the diversity of emotion that comes with a certain amount of distance from your grief. You're also depicting yourself as a more fully realized character, perhaps even one with a few blemishes. Try writing about a humorous incident that occurred when you were vulnerable, but you later came to appreciate the funny side of the situation.

Accepting What You Can Never Know

My father insisted in his later years that his great-aunt Jenny was cremated and her remains buried in a coffee can under the hedge that ran alongside his parents' house. All I know of Jenny is one sepia-tint photo of her, her chest solid and curved like the lid of an old-fashioned steamer trunk, her dark hair in an up-sweep and a proud smile as she stands beside her young niece and nephew at a paper moon on Coney Island in the nineteen teens. That niece grew up to be my father's mother. The nephew died young. Family legend says rheumatic fever, or the 1918 flu, or my mother's theory—Kostmann's syndrome—the illness that generations later appeared in Sarah, identified as a syndrome only a few years before her birth.

The coffee can story sounds unlikely to me, and as his illness progressed, my father's stories were sometimes an untraceable mix of dream and reality. There is no way to confirm what's either an oddball or alarming (or both) piece of my own history without knocking on what is now a stranger's front door and asking if I could please dig in their hedge for a coffee can.

I know the visible details of that photograph. Someone had

poked Jenny's eyes out. They're now rough-edged dark holes. From the look of the damage, a ballpoint pen might have been the instrument of destruction. I told my father that Jenny's photo was defaced when I got it (from whom, I don't recall) and he was flabbergasted. "We loved her," he said. "I can't believe anyone would do that."

The other fact is that the little boy, my great-uncle, was named Jack. My father was named for him. None of us in this generation or my father's generation knew that little boy, who died in the last year of the First World War.

The element of memoir here isn't who Jenny was, what happened to the first Jack, if Jenny's really interred in a coffee can, or who so deliberately went after her eyes in the photograph. There's grief here, without a doubt. An aunt and two little children have been consumed by the passage of time. A little boy died young, and the circumstances of his death are forgotten. A phantasmagorical burial—or my father's belief in one—in an otherwise socially upstanding neighborhood. And the defacement of the image of a woman remembered as beloved.

I have to accept that I will never know more about this story than what I can see with my own eyes. As a memoir writer, I wouldn't fictionalize the reasons the coffee can is or isn't there. Instead, what I can write about is what the story of Aunt Jenny and the coffee can tells me about my father's love for his great-aunt, whom I would never know. The damaged photograph brought me closer to my grandmother's childhood in New York, and showed me the only image I would ever see of an uncle who might have shared my sister Sarah's illness. For me, the empty space created by my lack of knowledge about what really happened to Aunt Jenny is filled with musings about how I wish I could have visited Coney Island in those ragtime days, what I do know in my own life about the streak of venom that ran through that branch of the family, and how it may have resulted in literal holes in an artifact of memory. And how I wish there were a way to know if that little boy had the same illness as my sister. I don't even know where he's buried. Surely not in a coffee can.

> TIP: Has working on your memoir uncovered a strange anecdote? Write about what that anecdote means to you personally and how it might work in your memoir's plot, particularly as an example of both "write what you don't know" and accepting that there are elements of the unknown in memoir that can, instead of being losses, become opportunities for reflection on story.

Your Writing Gives Strength to Others

Writing about our own losses takes emotional strength, but it creates strength, too, says Dr. Susan O'Doherty. It's helpful for a writer working on her grief memoir to know that there's "someone out there listening, that every story is valuable and will help someone else." There's a spark of communication with others in what you write, no matter if you're writing for your own family, for yourself, or a reader you may never meet.

Janisse Ray calls writing a healing action in itself. "Keep working on your own emotions as you write," she says. Being aware of your sadness or anger is one of many things, including involvement in bettering yourself and your world, that will carry a writer through the hard work. The last pages of Ray's most recent memoir, *Drifting into Darien: A Personal and Natural History of the Altamaha River*, suggest actions that a reader moved by the loss of landscape and place can do to make changes in themselves and in their world. The last one reads:

Be the keeper of whatever place you live.

"We're all experiencing a loss of a way of life," she explains. With her husband, she investigated practical skills that they both could learn that would serve their community. He trained to become an emergency medical technician, and they both became hospice volunteers. Together, they farm forty-six acres, and educate visitors about growing food.

"I'm not afraid of grief," she says. "It makes a person more clear."

I like the decisive way she says this. Facing grief on the page *does* make me more clear. I recognize that I've struggled with my feelings, and that writing my story helps me figure it out and reflect what I know back to myself as clearly as I can make it.

Seeing Yourself in Others' Stories

One of the first books I remember reading that looked head-on at grief was *Death Be Not Proud*, by John Gunther. First published in 1949, Gunther's book, named for the first stanza of John Donne's "Holy Sonnet X," was an homage to his son Johnny, who died as a teenager of a brain tumor.

I read the book at my grandparents' house over a school vacation. Their home was filled with big books, and as a seventh grader, I had already tried unsuccessfully to work my way through cinderblock-sized tomes like *The Oxford History of the American People*. This one, though, while hardback, heavy, and vaguely musty, was about a kid (what a relief) whose family life, like mine, was dominated by medical disaster. Johnny Gunther's story took place more than twenty years before ours, but the accessible language, the similarity to my own life, and the way the story unfolded hooked me.

Gunther was a journalist who specialized in stories that combined travel with culture and politics. *Death Be Not Proud* was, in a way, a travelogue of his son's courage and the family's unity during his fatal illness. The story took me on a journey, with unflinching scenic description and honest depictions of characters, and even though I knew at the outset that Johnny would not survive, the narrative had an arc: a beginning, middle, and end that kept me with the Gunthers on every page.

The same way that I read John Gunther's book and saw glimpses of my own experience in his family's struggle, readers can't help but look for aspects of themselves in your story, perhaps without even realizing that they're doing so. The story that you write is the narrative of your unique experience of grief, but your story and its spectrum of emotions should resonate with others. Your readers, no matter if they're your closest friends and family, your writing group, or people you'll never know, have lost someone or something important to them at some time. They, like you and me, read memoir because they seek reassurance about their experience.

Knowing You'll Want to Write About This Someday

As you write your way toward an ending, the ways that other writers work and the endings that they have crafted for their own stories will take on a sharper focus for you. Your writing has by now become a ritual of its own that you can rely on to help you see your world and your place in it. Think of your writing as a tool you can use to keep track of your coordinates on your ongoing map. Dr. Susan O'Doherty, the psychologist and author, observes that "one of the reasons we write is to stay alive and keep growing."

The urge you have to take notes, to write in your journal, and to establish the "I" self on the page is another sign of your acceptance of your story of grief. If or when grief touches your life again, you can face it with pen in hand, knowing that you can write through it. You've framed your experience for yourself and perhaps for future readers. Like you, they will someday look for memoirs that reflect back to them their own distinct losses and struggles to survive. You were like those readers at one time, turning to memoirs like Joan Didion's *The Year of Magical Thinking*, the story of her year immediately following the death of her husband and writing partner, John Gregory Dunne. A book like Kristen Iversen's memoir *Full Body Burden: Growing Up in the Nuclear Shadow of Rocky Flats* tells of growing up in a community built next to a secret nuclear weapons facility. And in *I Wore the Ocean in the Shape of a Girl*, Kelle Groom writes of the grief she experienced after giving her son up for adoption. Widowhood, environmental threats, the loss of a child, and so many other memoirs speak of grief experiences in the lives of these authors, their contemporary readers, and untold readers yet to come.

You might be done with your significant writing now that you've drafted the memoir you set out to write. You hope, and I hope, that the worst is over and that there will be no more grief in your life, but if there is, you'll find that the brain-spark and the journal habit are there, a welcomed and restorative habit. "You are the only one who can tell your story," author Sue William Silverman explained, when we talked about writing and loss. "Embrace the gift you're given: that you're a writer."

MY STORY:

These days, I make notes for an essay that's yet to come. I do this while I sit in an oncologist's waiting room, the same kind of place where my mother waited out long days with my two younger sisters. Now I wait out an afternoon with our mother. My sisters are not here, at least in body. They appear in my mind, my heart, and I wonder if Mom feels them nearby, too.

I am holding her hand. She has always been slim, and now that she's seventy-nine and thin, her hand is cold, and the skin on the back of her hand feels loose. She and I watch the wall-mounted television and listen to it bleat applause from a game show, then the mechanized sound of a lightning blaze that heralds the noon news. We share a women's magazine from the end table and compare our thoughts about the recipes, the fashions, the celebrities. Before I was born, she worked at a magazine like this one, answering the advice letters.

After the appointment, we walk carefully to her car. She is learning how to use her cane, and I hold her elbow and watch to make sure she doesn't stumble. "She should practice walking a straight line," her doctor told us. My mother and I count the steps, one, two, three, which reminds her of a jump rope rhyme from long ago.

One, two, three, O'Leary, my first name is Mary. The rhyme works better in my mother's Boston accent, and she pushes it to sound "really Boston." My mother was once a little girl playing jump rope at Merrymount School in Quincy, Massachusetts, where "O'Leary" rhymes with "Mary."

I have written the story of my sisters, our family, and me, but even when I wrote the ending to those pages I knew that the story of my life would continue. The impact of grief is looming again, but I've written it before. These days, as my mother and I talk about the news of the world and listen to some of her favorite music: Nina Simone, The Beatles, Frédéric Chopin, I know that I will write about that, too.

My mother will die. If I were to ask her to write an advice letter to me before she's gone, I would start my plea with "what do I do now? How will I accept this grief again, and who will help me to be the pragmatic woman you taught me to be?"

I'll craft that imaginary letter to you and to me, as grieving people and writers of memoir. We are allowed to feel sad, or frightened, or surprisingly happy at times in the midst of sorrow. Accept that you have the skill and desire to write about yourself and the people and places that you love, so you won't forget them.

The Next Step

1. Write an advice letter to yourself now that you're finishing a draft of your grief memoir. In it, tell yourself the ways that writing about a loss or losses in the past has given you insight into how you can accept a future loss and how you might write about it. Don't forget to remind yourself to use your senses, imagery, research, and above all, distance, before you put your hand into any new fire that might arise.

2. In what significant ways can you better your world, your home, your neighborhood, or your workplace? Is there an essay, a blog post, or an article for a local newspaper in that experience?

3. A Venn diagram is a visual way to compare the characteristics of two or more things. In order to write about how you've changed and remained the same since your grief began, create a Venn diagram. On a sheet of paper, draw two circles that partially overlap in the middle. Draw the circles large enough that they extend to each margin of the page. In one circle, jot down traits, images, phrases, anything you choose, from *before* your loss. In the other circle, jot down these same types of things for your life *after* your loss. In the section where the two circles overlap, write the observations that are consistent in your *before* and *after* lives. (You will almost certainly discover aspects in the middle that appear in one or both of the discrete circles.) Use these circles as a guide as you write about your journey through grief to acceptance and on to renewal. The diagram may also generate ideas for additional scenes.

4. Draft a potential ending to your memoir, then place it as the first section of your planned book or essay. How does this change the narrative? Does it imply reward for the reader and author, or does it give too much away?

5. Thinking back to your connective images, what metaphor is strongest in your memoir so far? In what ways can you integrate that imagery in the ending of your memoir?

6. In order to write an ending that promises reader reward and writer reward, go back through your manuscript draft and find material that describes you in the present day or near present looking back on your story. A moment of self-discovery or the juxtaposition between past and present selves is a good place to look. Perhaps there's a place in the story that describes the catalyst for writing your memoir. Use those ideas to craft an honest ending that closes the story on the page, but accepts that the story of your life goes on.

Six

RENEWAL

THE COURAGE IN THE LAST PAGE

Kathryn Rhett observes in her memoir *Near Breathing: A Memoir of a Difficult Birth* that a story is the passage through grief to possibility. Like that file cabinet of sorrow and jumbled memories that you've moved aside, grief is still there, but it no longer obstructs your path or your appraisal of what's already happened. You've renewed yourself as you wrote a bridge between who you were and who you have become—a writer who has told himself the story of his loss.

When I finished the manuscript of my memoir, I didn't write "the end" on the last page, like in the movies (it's always so easy in the movies) and rip the page from my typewriter (so much more photogenic than a laptop computer) with a flourish.

"*I* did this," I thought, impressed, measuring the manuscript's thickness against my thumb. I took my sorrow and love for my sisters, my parents, and I came to realize, myself, and told that story in a memoir that I was proud of.

I was proud of myself for telling the true story that I'd lived with for so long. I'd written a book in which I openly expressed sorrow, and was honest about unpleasant and grim times in my life. I had also written openly about joy, and satisfaction, and discovering that my voice and my identity were no longer silenced by my grief.

Because of this, I've added a sixth stage after the Kübler-Ross stages. Renewal is my own sixth stage of writing (and living) through grief, a stage that's purely about what happens to the grieving writer as she crafts and finishes her true story. One of the definitions for "renew" in the dictionary on my desk is "revive," or live again. In the creative effort you've made in writing your memoir of grief and loss, you have brought the important moments of your difficult past to life again, and survived them again. You have also given yourself the skill to keep on writing the continuing story of your life.

When Sue William Silverman talks about writing her two memoirs, she observes that, "I've taken [grief and trauma] out of myself, and it's in the book now." She compares writing about grief to removing the grief from inside yourself. It is painful, but "the hurting lessens [with] every word you take out of yourself." By writing your story of grief, you're making room in your life for a different story, one of change and renewal.

In this last chapter, you'll build the foundation for continuing to write, not only about losses in the past, but about celebrating who you are and honoring what's lost to you. You will explore the essay as a shorter form of writing nonfiction about grief, and will learn ways to build a community of mentors and mentees, no matter where you live. In this chapter, we'll also take a look at how you can benefit from writing conferences, reading groups, and how to answer that scalding question, "so, what's your memoir about?"

No Longer an Open Wound

The inherent strength and renewal that comes with writing honestly and compellingly about grief begins to take shape with the first words you write about your grief. Psychologist and author Dr. Susan O'Doherty agrees with many others who disagree with the concept of closure. Instead, she says she prefers the idea of "integration of the experience into your personality." Grief is no longer "an open wound that bleeds whenever we touch it."

Renewal is the stage when you recognize that you've written yourself into the desire to be fully alive. Fully alive isn't the same as constant ecstatic living, perpetual joy, or a rampaging case of the giggles. For the writer, it's a paraphrase of Henry James's famous quote, "A writer is someone on whom nothing is lost." You've written about your grief, and you're prepared to write about participating in the world after your loss.

Writing a grief memoir, like writing a grocery list, a course syllabus, or a work-flow plan, puts the business of living in order. For you as a writer, renewal means the joy and anticipation of a blank page and the easy glide of a new pen with exactly the right ink. Renewal is the willingness and even the thrill at moving forward and the confidence to recognize yourself on the page and in others' eyes.

Since *Invisible Sisters* was published, Susie and Sarah's friends have reached out to me in positive ways. A friend of Susie's sent me a copy of their third-grade class picture, which I had never seen. Another woman told me she had always wondered what happened to Susie. To her, Susie had been a classmate who "just disappeared" from school and never returned. Several of Sarah's friends have connected with me on social networks. We keep in touch, and we keep Sarah's memory alive in our relationship.

This link is bittersweet. My sisters' friends are grown men and women now, adults with professions, spouses, and kids. I can't help but think that Susie and Sarah should have had the lives and opportunities that their childhood friends do. That old cry of "unfair" will never leave me, and I know that my sisters' friends understand.

The person you've become has emerged from who you have been all along: a writer who has honored what you have lost and what you continue to grieve. You've written about who you are and what you can do because of your grief. You are celebrating your courage in revisiting that grief and writing your way through it. You have put your hand into the fire, and pulled it out whole.

Strength in Numbers

Renewal also comes from finding writers and readers immersed in themes and ideas similar to yours. They set an example for other writers through what they've done. You've set an example, too, in acting on your own desire to write about your loss and your renewal. No matter if you publish or not, make it your next step to get to know other writers. Writing a memoir about your grief isn't an egotistical act. When author Robin Hemley told me that he believes writing memoir "tends to humble us," I asked him to tell me more. He explained that writers of grief memoir, "face things that most people numb themselves to."

He's talking about the courage a writer musters as he confronts his loss and his changed identity. And he's talking about the community of writers and readers who understand the impact of the work you've done to write your story.

But the act of writing is solitary: no one can sit at your desk for you. This is why it's particularly important to know other people who understand what it's like to have had a day as creative or as shaky as yours. You're a lifeline for them, too. Just being able to give advice, even something you may consider simple like reminding a friend considering a grief memoir to jot down her memory of helping her father eat, or complimenting a fellow writer about a particularly memorable scene they've just written is a component of your own renewal.

But not all mentors are people you'll meet face-to-face. Many are writers whose work survives them although they have gone.

MY STORY:

I have a lot of writing mentors. Some are people I'll never meet, who don't know they're my mentors: Joan Didion, who writes of personal loss and cultural change with the even hand and precision of a diamond cutter, the novelist and short story writer Flannery O'Connor, who balances sorrow and humor with the same sly dazzle as a peacock unfurling his fan, or the late Lucy Grealy, whose memoir *Autobiography of a Face* set an impeccable standard for writing about physical damage and personal identity. There are so many writers at whose knees I would sit, notepad at the ready, if I could traverse time and space.

Not all of my mentors require breaking the time-space continuum. Many are professors and friends, others are writers and readers I've met through my own writing journey. My writing group consists of five friends, authors at various stages of their careers who mentor one another by paying close attention to each other's work, never hesitating to suggest ways to make a paragraph or even a sentence stronger, and genuinely celebrating each other's large and small successes.

Sometimes friends or students who are just beginning to write their stories of loss ask my advice. A man attending a workshop I'm leading about writing through grief writes when I give the group a prompt, but he can only weep when it's his turn to read aloud what's he's written. These writers don't recognize this yet, but they are on the path to being renewed. Just putting pen to paper, showing up at a workshop, writing the very beginning draft of a scene for a memoir—these people are committing acts of renewal in writing through their grief. The hardest work is already done, and that's living through the loss itself.

I read memoir voraciously, particularly grief memoirs.

I'm drawn to scholarly articles about understanding trauma, and about the changing science of treating the illnesses that have touched my family. I read first-person feature stories about innovative medical treatments, or service animals who help individuals with post-traumatic stress disorder or physical disabilities. I read about becoming a doctor. I read layperson's histories of cancer, the human stories behind cellular growth in a lab, a nonfiction account of a community's losses in a devastating fire.

In my reading, I'm touching base with what obsesses me, checking in to mark how I'm still changing and how the experience of surviving loss may change for others. Paraphrasing the late poet and essayist Adrienne Rich, survival is not static. As I continue to survive and change, I look behind and ahead for reminders of my progress, assessing my renewing self, facing who I am now and what I make of it.

As you continue to read in this genre and others, you build your identity as a writer. A writer who doesn't read greedily is a bit like a chef who limits his taste and only eats peanut butter and jelly sandwiches. Explore what other writers create that captures your imagination, and identify why their stories appeal to you.

The bibliography at the end of this book is a first step toward your collection of memoirs of grief, loss, or trauma. These books are the works of writers who have taken on similar subjects to yours. You can also take the recommendations of writers and readers who you trust in your writing group, your family, and among your friends. Browse the shelves of a bookstore or library and ask the bookseller or the librarian what they recommend. The book review sections in newspapers and magazines are unfortunately dwindling, but many publications continue to dedicate thought-provoking care and insight to reviewing books. There are also a wealth of opinions in book-lovers' sites online.

In her introduction to the anthology *Survival Stories: Memoirs of Crisis*, Rhett writes that in memoirs about depression, lost friendships, broken marriages, illness, and death, she found what she calls essential discoveries in a writer's life. In them, she recognized that she wanted to read about people in the jarring moments of their lives. She experienced that fundamental connection that comes from reading about how other people have made it through their deepest troubles.

Birds of a Feather

This fellowship of writers—the "club" in which you're a member—has a not-so-secret signal. The signal is found in the content of our memoirs and essays. It's in the questions asked by members of the audience at author readings and writers' conferences: "Was this book difficult to write?" or "Do you feel differently about your loss now that you've written about it?" These questions come up because, like you before you started this journey, the person asking them is wondering if he can put his hand back into the fire.

You can find other writers with whom you'll feel comfortable more easily than you might think. Writers' conferences are everywhere: large cities, small towns, even vacation retreats. Some are so academic and crowded that the hotel lobby during registration is as loud as a hydroelectric dam. Three days of discussions about craft and technique overlap with star-power readings, and famous writers mingle with graduate students and writing professors, many of whom are highly regarded. While this is a thrilling event for some writers, others might call a weekend like this not for the faint of heart. But most conferences are smaller, and participation feels as relaxed as browsing a community bake sale. Conferences like these tend to take place in church social halls, libraries, and community centers. Even these smaller conferences bring in "big name" writers as well as local and regional writers. Often, agents and editors will be in attendance, available to discuss your idea with you or listen to a short "pitch" about your memoir.

But taking time out of your busy schedule to attend a writers' conference, even for a day, can be an obstacle if you live with a demanding job and family obligations. You may find that joining a local book club can have similar benefits, especially a group that welcomes a visit by the author of the book the group is currently reading. (An author's virtual visit by conference call or video streaming is a great way to facilitate a personal talk about writing with the author.) This way, new writers and the visiting established writer have a chance that they might not have in a large conference setting to meet and talk about the issue at hand: ways to write memorably about what you can't forget.

Join a writers' group or start a writers' group. You'll find that bulletin boards (and websites) connected with your local library, independent bookstore, community centers, churches, synagogues, and colleges are good places to reach out. Even if the group's sum total is you and one other person, establish a schedule that includes a time to exchange your work in progress, and another time to meet and discuss the writing. Sharing work and commentary over the Internet is a great choice for busy people or a collection of writers separated by distance. Online writers' groups and writing classes exist all over the world, and you can look them up through an Internet search.

As you work with a writers' group, know your tender spots and your strong spots. Join or create a group with like-minded writers who are your peers in their craft. Mix memoirists and novelists in a writing group: fiction writers can offer insight into plot and character techniques, and you can give tips about research and openness. They'll write differently than you— that's voice—but in a convivial writers' group, every member is open to the craft of reading and writing about grief, loss, change, and renewal.

On Being Seen

Darin Strauss writes in *Half a Life: A Memoir* about going to the movies with friends the same afternoon as his car accident. The girl he hit was in the hospital. He did not yet know that she had died. His excursion to the movies wasn't glib; his parents suggested it to take his mind off the accident. In the memoir, the present-day character of Darin argues with himself about why he went, and recounts his guilt, remorse, and uncertainty about whether he should visit the girl's hospital room. In the theater lobby, he encounters a friend, whose attempts to make a joke about the events earlier in the day horrify and unsettle Darin.

> I felt panicky and bright and swollen: hugely sad, acutely seen. I slouched away, tucked myself into the theater's dark, and had a sense of being extinguished.

It's that act of writing about the grief and its accompanying confusion, the feeling of being "acutely seen" that "allows us to de-extinguish the parts of ourselves that we'd had eradicated by loss," Strauss told me. "It forces you to face yourself."

When my husband, Mickey, was offered the opportunity to read part of his memoir-in-progress at a local reading series, he jumped at the chance. On the nominal level, his memoir in-progress is about dating, an activity where anxiety and misunderstanding can create a kind of grief of their own. On the substantive level, though, he's writing about growing up frustrated by the religious and cultural constraints he remembered his parents requiring, and the very real grief that a single rebellious act ultimately caused him, his family, and close friends. The reading series was a monthly event at a café where professional and amateur nonfiction writers read short works to a crowd composed largely of friends and friends of friends, all of whom are enthusiastic readers and writers. We're regulars there, and everyone was in a good mood. The orders for wine, coffee, and snacks kept the waiters moving.

He chose to read part of a chapter in which he, like many nineteen-sixties and seventies-era American Jewish children, was educated about the Holocaust. Many of their grandparents knew these lessons firsthand. A few had survived the war as children, others knew of family members who had died. Mickey wrote about what it was like for him to watch films in Sunday school that depicted the starved bodies in the concentration camps, and how looking back on this as an adult, he came to feel that the terrifying lesson forced a responsibility to uphold a culture on children too young to make sense of it.

At the café, Mickey went to the podium. The audience applauded, and then went back to eating and drinking casually as they listened first to the emcee, and then to him. I sat with friends. We were silent and proud, watching him turn pages, listening to the strength in his soft, calm voice. He read:

> I never asked my parents why they didn't want me to date shiksas, because I already knew the answer. All parents want their children to date their own kind, but Jewish parents had an extra reason why it was essential that Jewish boys procreated only with Jewish girls. That reason was the Holocaust.
>
> The Holocaust made my parents more paranoid about the survival of the Jews. They were young adults living in America during World War Two. The Holocaust happened to Eastern European Jews during their lifetimes. If the systematic murder of six million Jewish men, women, and children didn't make you xenophobic, then nothing would.

His voice faltered. He stopped, cleared his throat, and started again. He had come face-to-face with the crucial moment in his piece for the first time, even though he'd rehearsed his reading and written and rewritten the chapter. When he practiced his reading in a mirror, he hadn't predicted the effect his own words would have on him. His honesty about an excruciating topic that he grieved as a child and found that he still grieved as an adult would affect him and his listeners in an unexpected way. As he read aloud, he confronted the substance of the piece: his own mixed emotions about wanting to forget, and the importance of never forgetting a deep loss that he had come to understand.

At Sunday school, my classmates and I were shown Holocaust films. We bore witness to the piles of dead bodies, the emaciated prisoners, and the lamps made from human skin, all in grainy black and white that made it even more grim, like home movies from hell.

Mickey's throat seemed to clog. He stopped reading, and I saw that he was teary eyed. I wanted to run to him, but I stayed put, holding my breath and hurting for him. Slowly, he began to read again.

Over the years, we were shown the Holocaust films many times. There was no age limit; you didn't have to be this tall to see the human devastation. Instead, we were required to watch the horror again and again so that we would never forget. Our elders wanted the images to be tattooed on our brains.

The chatty buzz in the room had stopped. The audience was riveted. It seemed to me that each of the two dozen or so people in the room had been suddenly transported to their own moments of heartbreak, no matter what their culture or upbringing had been.

Mickey left the stage to applause, and made his way back to our table through a crowd of back-slapping and friendly hugs. When he sat down, he was shocked and pleased.

"I didn't know that was in there," he said, amazed. He knew that his *sentences* were "in there," but what he hadn't expected was the power in his true story of grief. Reading the work to others allowed him to experience the full impact and art of his writing. He was surprised to find that he was renewed. His personal story, even with grim and defiant moments, mattered.

Writing about your grief can be just as powerful if your memoir is only for your eyes and ears. No one else needs to know that you've put your hand back into the fire and pulled it out in order to write. You know it. And that's renewal.

MY STORY:

It took me fifteen years before I saw the baby steps I had taken toward claiming my identity at my sister Sarah's shiva. I realized as I wrote that I'd made those steps and what they had meant to my ability to survive. The scene reads, in part, like this.

> Be careful what you wish for, my mother warns . . .
> She laughs when she says this. She is a habitual
> wisher, on pennies found face up or face down,
> and on loose eyelashes caught with a fingertip. My
> mother dries the wishbones from chickens, and to-
> gether we pull the brittle Y shapes apart. Silently, I
> wish to be fully alive, while my mother wishes for
> my desires to come true.
>
> In my worst moods, I wonder why I am alive.
> Illness hid in my sisters' cells, but no disease has
> emerged from mine. You are alive just to be alive,
> I imagine Sarah saying. Susie, forever eight years
> old, concurs. You are alive because you are alive.

My ongoing deep grief dwells in the same place as my acceptance of my survival. Recognizing that, and writing what I believe my sisters would tell me now if they could, renewed me.

Writing the Smaller Canvas

Writing a literary essay is an active way to find your memoir's ending. You can also write essays as warm-ups to your revisions, when you develop the outcomes of ideas and images that you didn't initially feel were the right fit, but call out to you now that you have a sense of your whole manuscript. Sometimes essays are new pieces all their own. Many memoirs that you love and will come to love were written by authors who first wrote through their own grief in the essay form. Sometimes the essay suited what they wanted to say and how they wanted to say it. Others found that after they'd written an essay or two, they wanted to expand or combine their essays into longer work. Michael Steinberg, author of *Still Pitching* and founding editor of *Fourth Genre: Explorations in Nonfiction,* says that writing for and reading literary magazines are a writer's apprenticeship. He told me that he believes that writers "learn in the short form." I know this is true for me as a writer. Writing an essay lets me try out the flow of new ideas.

Author Dinty W. Moore is founder and editor of the online magazine *Brevity: A Journal of Concise Literary Nonfiction,* in which essays can be no longer than 750 words. What Moore looks for in essays about loss are works that go beyond the idea that loss is painful. What catches his eye as an editor is a piece that he describes as one that, "tries to extend our knowledge of grief or illness."

Here's an example from Rebecca McClanahan's essay, "Loving Bald Men," which appeared in *Brevity* in the fall of 2002.

Months since my nephew slid otter-slick into the doctor's hand, I anoint his head with baby oil, brailling his fate: Is baldness in his future? The first time I touched a bald man's head I was a grown woman, and I read in the elegant bones of his skull *my* future for the next few hours at least. Bare of tuft or leaf or feather, sleek mountain summit, undisguised, evident, in a word: *bold,* as in *bald,* both arising out of *shining, white.*

In this almost musical essay that begins with the image of an infant, glides over the baldness of a man's head and, it's later implied, the beginnings of her own, McClanahan touches on a subject that she wrestles with in much of her writing: beginnings and endings, losses and joy.

She uses the noun "Braille" as a verb—"brailling"—to describe reading the future with her fingers on a man's bald head as a blind person might touch the raised dots of a page written in Braille.

When we talked, McClanahan compared writing an essay to painting on "a smaller canvas" than writing a book, but a canvas on which an author "can still do different kinds of strokes." Even a small canvas invites the person writing a grief memoir to do work that expresses an aspect of their story. A successful essay, McClanahan believes, is "well crafted, intellectually and emotionally moving, and whole within itself."

An essay that's "whole within itself" adheres to the structure of beginning, middle, and end, but in a very tightly focused way that still makes room for a loose, even exploratory approach in language or form. "I want to feel the gears shift," McClanahan said, adding that those changes shouldn't be obvious or clunky. "You can't end a memoir [or an essay] where you start it. Something has to shift."

In the preface to her collection, *The Riddle Song And Other Rememberings,* McClanahan writes about exactly this phenomenon.

The following essays evolved over the space of many years. Each was shaped as a complete, independent work, but over time it became clear that, taken together, the essays formed a whole larger than the sum of individual parts . . . Like the recurring lines of "The Riddle Song," the folk tune my mother used to sing to us from the driver's seat of one station wagon or another, the essays loop back upon themselves. Images resurface, places are revisited, the same people keep showing up at the door of every tale. And the same questions keep asking themselves.

If you think about the idea of "distance" from earlier in this book, that's the "many years" in the first sentence of McClanahan's preface. Writing grief memoir, even in the essay form, often needs distance, revision, and the author's ear for what's right and what's not quite there yet in her own work.

MY STORY:

I didn't originally consider the story of my family and my sisters' lives and deaths as a full-length memoir. I loved reading memoir, and for most of my life have been drawn to any true story about illness, family, and loss. I wanted to know—needed to know—what those authors knew about how to live after loss. Maybe they could show me how they did it.

Invisible Sisters began as essays: self-contained shorter explorations that developed into longer narrative pieces, some for publication, others just for me. Every essay made cautious probes into what I hadn't yet confronted in my writing or in my life: how I had come to be a woman who outlived her sisters, and what that would mean for how I chose to experience my future.

In an essay called "Daughter Cells," named both for

the product of cell division and for my question to have or not have children, I wrote,

> Open my veins and coax information out. Find the answer to my parents' anguish and tell me if I will face the same. Isolate the random error in our genetic code as if you were fishing macaroni letters from a bowl of alphabet soup. Because I knew early on that a lab technician was looking for mutations in my family's cells, I believed that at our most primitive level, my family was different from others. If we had a mutation then we would be freaks. Almost immediately, I became fascinated by stories about Chang and Eng, twins conjoined by a band of flesh at their chests, or with tales of General Tom Thumb and his bride Lavinia Warren. Leafing through my parents' book of Diane Arbus photographs, I happened on a portrait of lunkish and tragic Eddie Carmel, who at a purported nine feet tall, towered over his stunned parents. I opened the book to "A Jewish giant at home with his parents in the Bronx, NYC 1970" over and over again, wondering how Eddie could sleep comfortably in bed and if his back ached from bending so low to walk through doorways.

As I look back on this essay more than ten years after I wrote it, I can see how I was locating the themes that defined me. I followed those themes in the idea of genetic "freaks" like Tom Thumb and his bride, dwarves who appeared in P. T. Barnum's shows in the middle of the nineteenth century, and alternately, Eddie Carmel, the "Jewish Giant," and my sisters and me—two of us ill with almost diametrically opposed illnesses, and me, so far physically unharmed.

As a writer, I was fortunate, because this essay was accepted by a literary magazine, which gave me the confidence to keep writing, going deeper into the fire with every attempt.

Reigniting the Brain-Spark

As your writing continues, the brain-spark habit doesn't stop. Stray thoughts and ideas might ignite from what you've written, sending you down a path toward writing a second or third full-length piece, a piece of narrative journalism, a short story or poem, a young adult book, or even a graphic novel or memoir. You've started to accept that your story is part of you.

Dr. Pennebaker observes that human beings "naturally need to understand complex experiences. [B]y talking to other people you get their perspective, and they understand you better. Putting [the complex experience] into words helps you come to terms with it." In *The Secret Life of Pronouns*, he writes,

> Exploring emotional topics demands that people look inward (as we see by their increasing use of first-person singular I-words). It helps them to organize their thoughts and construct more meaningful explanations or stories of their lives (as seen in the increasing use of cognitive words). By tracking the ways people write about their traumas, we are witnessing how they are changing in their thinking.

Natasha Trethewey says that for her, writing—"using language"—holds back the inevitable loss that comes with time. "All writing for me is writing about loss," she says. "You're writing about what's already gone."

How to Build a Monument

My friend Beth burned her journals. She incinerated six months' worth of writing in a pyre on the concrete beside her apartment complex swimming pool. She was making big changes in her life, and felt that she needed a fresh start. The idea of burning journals seemed to me a reckless act that would create grief, not liberation. Another friend had done a similar thing a few years earlier. To my astonishment, students in workshops have told me that they've burned journals, too. It's a cleansing act for many people, a scorched-earth solution to a past they are ready to be free of. My friends, and I imagine my students, too, burned their journals to commemorate the end of one creative process and the freedom to start a new one. Pleased with their final product, they memorialized the drafts as ashes.

You can burn your journals if you like, but I can't bring myself to do the same for mine. I'm both a pack rat and a writer whose journals are a vital, as in necessary-for-living, part of my work. But I'm also a writer who loves metaphor. Hearing these stories of destruction got me thinking about what happens after we've looked back on our pasts and drawn from them what we need to help us understand and write in a forward-moving way about our grief. I call the hardest parts of that writing "sticking your hand back into a fire" for a reason. That experience can be as raw as a burn, but the grief itself is like a flame: ephemeral, vaporous, ever at the ready.

Perhaps people who burn their journals are creating their own ritual, and turning the past into something they can say good-bye to as the ashes float away. The Jewish tradition after a death is to light a *yarzheit* candle every year on the anniversary of the loss. The candle's flame commemorates the deceased loved one's soul, as it does in a variety of other traditions.

Burning a candle while contemplating a loss is a monument, but it's a fleeting one: a *yarzheit* candle burns for only twenty-four hours.

Natasha Trethewey writes about the physical monuments of her home landscape in *Beyond Katrina*: monuments to Confederate soldiers, a Plexiglas box on a town green filled with found objects like dolls, clothing, and a clock—debris from the daily lives lost to Katrina—and the ancient live oak trees that withstood the storm. To her, writing about loss is a monument of the best kind. "Writing is a generative thing," she told me. "You've had to make something out of the loss, and so what you've done is created a monument that is ongoing each time the piece will be read. It's . . . a tribute to renewal."

So let me leave you with a scene from a true story in the making.

It's late on a sunny weekday afternoon, and I'm heading home from a day of teaching. As I leave the college campus, I decide to pop into the school bookstore. I have no pressing reason to be there, I just want to browse, and so I go straight for the art supplies. Notebooks are on sale, and my faculty ID provides an added discount. I snap up a sketchbook, hardbound in black and small enough to fit into my messenger bag. Emotions, people, and places are shifting in my life, as always, and I feel the need to write what's on my mind.

In the car, before I turn on the ignition and head out into the gathering traffic, this is what I write.

Not lost, but found.

In my imagination, I hand the nearly blank book to you, a student, a reader, a friend, and a member of that fellowship of grief writers.

"Your turn," I say, easing us through a green light. "Go ahead and write about what you want to come next."

MY STORY:

Epilogue

As this book went into production, my mother died. She had been living with metastasizing cancer for nearly three years. My husband and I were with her when she died, in her home, as she had wanted.

My hand was in the fire again while I wrote this book. As my mother's physical well-being diminished, I wrote parts of the last chapters at her side. I thought about how I will give myself permission to write honestly about my life as it continues without my mother. I reflected on what angers me, and I began to contemplate the bargains I will make with myself and with my own new true stories.

The journals I kept these past few years include dour and lively moments. Some pages record medications prescribed and appointments scheduled. Others are notes from my visit to a museum with a good friend. There's a poorly rendered sketch of my view from a train window. On another page, Mom's elegant, narrow handwriting demonstrates a long division problem, all these years after I never quite got the hang of it. Just skimming those journals shows me that I had already begun to take care of myself.

Writing this epilogue is one of many steps toward acceptance.

One of the last things we did together was celebrate the first page proofs of *Braving the Fire*. The pages came three days before she died, and I brought them to her house so she could see the book's progress. Opening that package was a courageous act for both of us, not only because of the excitement in seeing a book nearly finished, but because we knew without saying so that she would never see the final book. We read a few pages at her dining table and drank ginger tea, one of the foods she still had a taste for. We put our hands into the fire together that day, and it burned bright and hot on the next chapters of my story.

THE NEXT STEP

1. The fellowship of writing about grief begins with the bibliography of works discussed in these pages. This list is by no means comprehensive. Memoirs of grief and trauma extend all the way back to the Confessions of St. Augustine, written around 398 CE, and new works are available all the time. To find them, read book reviews in magazines and online, and make notes to yourself about books you might want to read next in this field. Add to your notes as you discover other works that are helpful to you. Consider these books, essays, and articles as a membership roster for that loose fellowship of writers who put their true stories of grief and renewal to paper. And when you're ready, add yourself to it, no matter if there's a single copy of your memoir just for you, or if you someday hope to see your name on a bestseller list.

2. Write a list of what you fear will be the worst that happens when someone reads your work. Now write a list of rewarding things that might happen as a result of your work being read.

3. If you find that it's hard to carve out time to write, Janisse Ray suggests listing ten sensory images that capture a particular experience. You can expand on these when you have the time. Taking a few minutes to jot down significant images, tastes, or smells from your surroundings will help you write more thoroughly later.

4. Imagine that you're getting ready to attend a writers' conference where you will tell people about your memoir,

either as a formal pitch to an agent or editor, or in conversation with fellow writers. In film pitches, plots are given in succinct "log lines" that get right to the point in stating the protagonist/antagonist conflict and how the story's outcome is reached. As an example, a logline for the fairy tale "Cinderella," might be:

> Neglected Cinderella can't attend the Prince's ball because her jealous stepsisters force her to stay home. She is surprised by her fairy godmother who magically outfits her and sends her to the ball in a carriage, but warns her to return before the spell breaks at midnight. Cinderella enchants the Prince, but loses a glass slipper as she hurries home. The prince brings the shoe to every woman in his kingdom until he finds her. As they marry, Cinderella forgives her cruel stepsisters.

Try out the clarity of your pitch by filling in this sentence:

> A (main character) wants to B, but encounters C (antagonist or antagonistic event), so (or but or the coordinating conjunction of your choice) the main character does (or whatever verb is appropriate to the action) D (one of your major plot points) that changes him or her in E way. (Remember to create a rewarding, forward-moving ending.)

6. List five activities that make you feel renewed. That list might include starting a new journal or sketchpad, reading (no matter if the subject is unrelated to your own writing), gardening or cooking, or overhearing a phrase that sparks your imagination. Post that list in your writing space or in your journal. Consult it regularly and add to it as you discover new ways to invigorate your writing and your perspective.

Author's Note

There are so many excellent memoirs and essays about loss and grief, and throughout the writing of this book, I wished for the room to include them all, but as it should be, that list never stops growing. The authors and other professionals interviewed for this book have each had profound influences on my writing, but do not necessarily endorse the Kübler-Ross "Five Stages of Grief" as a coping method.

My thanks to the writers, friends, and mentors with whom I was able to speak for this book, and to those who have shaped my writing, either directly or indirectly. I'm honored to look toward your work for guidance. Thank you, too, to the writers who so beautifully express our changing human condition every day.

Select Bibliography

Adiele, Faith. *Meeting Faith: An Inward Odyssey*. New York: W. W. Norton & Co. 2004.

Agee, James. *A Death in the Family*. New York: McDowell Obolensky. 1957.

Aldrich, Marcia. *Companion to an Untold Story*. Athens, GA: The University of Georgia Press. 2012.

Aristotle. *Poetics*. New York: Dover Publications. 1997.

Bauby, Jean-Dominique. *The Diving Bell and the Butterfly*. New York: Knopf. 1997.

Bayley, John. *Elegy for Iris*. New York: St. Martin's Press. 1999.

Beard, Jo Ann. *The Boys of My Youth*. New York: Back Bay Books. 1999.

Beasley, Sandra. *Don't Kill the Birthday Girl: Tales from an Allergic Life*. New York: Crown. 2011.

Bechdel, Alison. *Fun Home: A Family Tragicomic*. New York: Houghton Mifflin Harcourt. 2006.

Braestrup, Kate. *Here If You Need Me: A True Story*. New York: Back Bay Books. 2008.

Brown, Ian. *The Boy in the Moon: A Father's Journey to Understand His Extraordinary Son*. New York: St. Martin's Press. 2009.

Didion, Joan. *The Year of Magical Thinking*. New York: Knopf. 2005.

Fernandez, Benedict. *Countdown to Eternity*. Pittsburgh: Manchester Craftsmen's Guild. 1993.

Flynn, Nick. *Another Bullshit Night in Suck City: A Memoir.* New York: W. W. Norton & Co. 2004.

Foreman, Gene. *The Ethical Journalist: Making Responsible Decisions in Pursuit of News.* Hoboken, NJ: Wiley-Blackwell. 2009.

Fourth Genre: Explorations in Nonfiction (biannual journal). Michigan State University Press.

Fragoso, Margaux. *Tiger, Tiger: A Memoir.* New York: Farrar, Straus and Giroux. 2011.

Frank, Anne. *The Diary of a Young Girl.* New York: Pocket Books. 1953.

Frazier, Ian. *Family.* New York: Farrar, Straus and Giroux. 1994.

Frazier, Ian. "Looking for My Family" in *Inventing the Truth: The Art and Craft of Memoir.* Ed. Zinsser, William. New York: Mariner Books. 1998.

Fuller, Alexandra. *Don't Let's Go to the Dogs Tonight: An African Childhood.* New York: Random House. 2003.

Gallagher, Dorothy. *How I Came Into My Inheritance: And Other True Stories.* New York: Random House. 2001.

Gilsdorf, Ethan. *Fantasy Freaks and Gaming Geeks: An Epic Quest for Reality Among Role Players, Online Gamers, and Other Dwellers of Imaginary Realms.* Guilford, CT: The Lyons Press. 2009.

Grealy, Lucy. *Autobiography of a Face.* New York: Harper Perennial. 1994.

Groom, Kelle. *I Wore the Ocean in the Shape of a Girl: A Memoir.* New York: Free Press. 2011.

Guest, Paul. *One More Theory About Happiness: A Memoir.* New York: Ecco Press. 2010.

Gunther, John. *Death Be Not Proud.* New York: Harper Perennial. 1998.

Handler, Jessica. *Invisible Sisters: A Memoir.* New York: Public Affairs. 2009.

Handler, Jessica. "Daughter Cells" in *Body & Soul: Narratives of Healing from Ars Medica.* Ed. Crawford, Allison, Rex Kay, Allan Peterkin, Robin Roger, and Ronald Ruskin, with Aaron Orkin. Toronto: University of Toronto Press. 2012.

Hemley, Robin. *A Field Guide for Immersion Writing: Memoir, Journalism, and Travel.* Athens, GA: University of Georgia Press. 2012.

Hemley, Robin. *Nola: A Memoir of Faith, Art, and Madness.* St. Paul, MN: Graywolf Press. 1998.

Hemley, Robin. *Do-Over! In Which a Forty-Eight-Year-Old Father of Three Returns to Kindergarten, Summer Camp, the Prom, and Other Embarrassments.* New York: Little, Brown, and Company. 2009.

Hood, Ann. *Comfort: A Journey Through Grief.* New York: W. W. Norton & Co. 2009.

Huber, Sonya. *Cover Me: A Health Insurance Memoir.* Lincoln, NE: University of Nebraska Press. 2010.

Iversen, Kristen. *Full Body Burden: Growing Up in the Nuclear Shadow of Rocky Flats.* New York: Crown. 2012.

Joyce, James. *A Portrait of the Artist as a Young Man.* New York: Dover. 1994.

Karr, Mary. *The Liars' Club.* New York: Penguin. 1995.

Kübler-Ross, Elisabeth. *On Death and Dying.* New York: MacMillan. 1970.

Leone, Marianne. *Knowing Jesse: A Mother's Story of Grief, Grace, and Everyday Bliss.* New York: Simon & Schuster. 2010. (Also known as *Knowing Jesse: A Mother's Story.*)

Lewis, Clive Staples. *A Grief Observed.* New York: Bantam Books. 1967.

Mairs, Nancy. *Plaintext: Deciphering a Woman's Life.* New York: Perennial. 1987.

Martin, Lee. *From Our House: A Memoir.* New York: Dutton. 2000.

McClanahan, Rebecca. *The Riddle Song and Other Rememberings.* Athens, GA: University of Georgia Press. 2002.

McClanahan, Rebecca. "Loving Bald Men." *Brevity 12.* Fall, 2002. https:www.creativenonfiction.org/brevity

McElmurray, Karen Salyer. *Surrendered Child: A Birth Mother's Journey.* Athens, GA: University of Georgia Press. 2004.

Moore. Dinty W. *Between Panic and Desire.* Lincoln, NE: University of Nebraska Press. 2008.

Nabokov, Vladimir. *Speak, Memory.* New York: Knopf. 1999.

O'Doherty, Susan. *Getting Unstuck Without Coming Unglued: A Woman's Guide to Unblocking Creativity.* Berkeley, CA: Seal Press. 2007.

Pennebaker, James. *The Secret Life of Pronouns: What Our Words Say About Us.* New York: Bloomsbury Press. 2011. www.secretlifeofpronouns.com

"Portaits of Grief" *New York Times.* September 14, 2001–December 31, 2001.

Ray, Janisse. *Drifting into Darien: A Personal and Natural History of the Altamaha River.* Athens, GA: University of Georgia Press. 2011.

Ray, Janisse. *Ecology of a Cracker Childhood.* Minneapolis, MN: Milkweed Editions. 1999.

Rhett, Kathryn. *Near Breathing: A Memoir of a Difficult Birth.* Pittsburgh: Duquesne University Press. 1997.

Rhett, Kathryn, ed. *Survival Stories: Memoirs of Crisis.* New York: Anchor Books. 1997.

Roberts, Gene, and Hank Klibanoff. *The Race Beat: The Press, the Civil Rights Struggle, and the Awakening of a Nation.* New York: Vintage Books. 2007.

Roueché, Berton. *Eleven Blue Men and Other Narratives of Medical Detection.* New York: Berkley Medallion. 1965.

Sebold, Alice. *Lucky: A Memoir.* New York: Scribner's. 1999.

Shapiro, Dani. *Devotion: A Memoir.* New York: Harper. 2010.

Silverman, Sue William. *Because I Remember Terror, Father, I Remember You.* Athens, GA: University of Georgia Press. 1999.

Steinberg, Michael. *Still Pitching: A Memoir.* East Lansing, MT: Michigan State University Press. 2003.

Strauss, Darin. *Half a Life.* New York: Random House. 2010.

Tea, Michelle. *The Chelsea Whistle: A Memoir.* Berkeley, CA: Seal Press. 2002.

Thomas, Abigail. *A Three Dog Life: A Memoir.* New York: Harcourt, Inc. 2006.

Thomas, Abigail. *Safekeeping: Some True Stories from a Life.* New York: Anchor Books. 2001.

Thomas, Lewis. *The Lives of a Cell: Notes of a Biology Watcher.* New York: Viking. 1974.

Trethewey, Natasha. *Beyond Katrina: A Meditation on the Mississippi Gulf Coast.* Athens, GA: University of Georgia Press: 2010.

Walls, Jeannette. *The Glass Castle: A Memoir.* New York: Scribner. 2005.

Weber, Katharine. *The Memory of All That: George Gershwin, Kay Swift, and My Family's Legacy of Infidelities.* New York: Crown. 2011.

Weintraub, Amy. *Yoga Skills for Therapists: Effective Practices for Mood Management.* New York: W. W. Norton & Co. 2012.

Welty, Eudora. *One Writer's Beginnings.* New York: Warner Books. 1984.

White, Neil. *In the Sanctuary of Outcasts: A Memoir.* New York: William Morrow. 2009.

Wickersham, Joan. *The Suicide Index: Putting My Father's Death in Order.* New York: Mariner Books. 2009.

Woolf, Virginia. *On Being Ill.* Ashfield, MA: Paris Press. 2007.

Zasky, Jason. "Haunted by the Failures of His Youth, a Middle-Aged Husband and Father Goes back to School—Elementary School" *Failure Magazine.* 2012. http: www.http://failuremag.com/feature /article/do-over/

Index

photographs, 146, 148
  of Handler's father, 149–51
  in *From Our House*, 151–52
Plaintext: Deciphering a Woman's Life
  (Mairs), 56
plot
  development, 39
  map of, 79–81
  nominal level of, 45, 83, 217
  in stories, 33
  substantive level of, 45–46, 83,
    217
point of view, 57–61
A Portrait of the Artist as a Young Man
  (Joyce), 39
"Portraits of Grief" series, of Scott,
  182
protagonist, 181
  anger and, 40–41, 45
  endings, in memoirs, and, 94
  point of view, 61
provable truth, 156–57

*The Race Beat: The Press, the Civil
  Rights Struggle, and the Awakening
  of a Nation* (Klibanoff), 139
racism, 109–10
Ray, Janisse, 6, 53–54, 79, 153, 186,
  202, 229
religion, 109–10
remembering, 25, 50
renewal, 209–30
  grief stage, 5
  monuments and, 226–27
  writers' conferences for, 215–16,
    229–30
  writers' fellowships for, 212–17
reporters, 138–43
research, 127–38
  medical records, 134–37
  for *From Our House*, 142–43
  practical experts, 131–32
  of sensory experiences, 128
  as time travel, 127–31

resonant ending, 95–96
resources, libraries as, 143–46
revision, of writing, 187
Rhett, Kathryn, 16, 77–78, 82, 125,
  169, 209, 215
  on denial, 17
  on notebook, 174
Rich, Adrienne, 214
"The Riddle Song: A Twelve-Part
  Lullaby" (McClanahan), 112
*The Riddle Song And Other
  Rememberings* (McClanahan),
  222
Roueché, Berton, 2
rule-based thinking, 155

*Safekeeping: Some True Stories from a
  Life* (Thomas, Abigail), 21–22,
  67
safety shield, for depression, 181
Scott, Janny, 182
screenwriting, 83, 86–87
Sebold, Alice, 56
second person, writing in, 58
*The Secret Life of Pronouns: What Our
  Words Say About Us* (Pennebaker),
  159, 166–67, 225
self-discovery, 11
sensory experiences, 128
sensory imagery, 125
Shapiro, Dani, 190
signal phrases, in memoirs, 62, 66
signs, 120–21
Silverman, Sue William, 6, 54, 158,
  166, 189, 205, 210
  on closure, 190
Songs of Innocence and of Experience
  (Blake), 55
sparse dialogue, 65
Speak, Memory (Nabokov), 117–18
Steinberg, Michael, 58–59, 62,
  183–84, 221
Still Pitching (Steinberg), 58, 62,
  183–84, 221